GRAND PRIX

SHOEI
Marlboro
LONGINES
Agip
28
digital
WEBER
MAGNETI MARELLI
GOODYEAR

Marlb
USF&G

GRAND PRIX

CONTENTS

First published in 1987 by
Octopus Books Limited, Grosvenor Street, London, England

ISBN 0 86273 398 7
Printed in Spain

Marlboro
Marlboro
rlboro
GOODYEAR

Beba
Coca-Cola
GOOD YEAR
Shell
BOSS
Marlboro

HERCULES
1
Prost
BOSS
Marlboro
Marlboro
Shell

INTRODUCTION

The sport of Formula 1 racing is recognised as a leading trend-setter in matters of technical excellence in the world today. Continuous technological breakthroughs in the past decade have led to faster, safer and more interesting sport for the millions who watch every race, and the trend for innovation will, I believe, continue – to everyone's benefit.

The role of the grand prix driver may have changed a great deal over the years, but his commitment to a whole range of skills has not. More than ever, today's driver has to be able not only to identify with the rapidly changing technical advances but to deal with the new world of promotion and public life. When I am not racing for the Marlboro McLaren TAG Turbo Team I spend a great deal of time testing the cars in an effort to improve our performance, and then of course there are numerous promotional undertakings with our many commercial sponsors around the world.

For the public in general, an overall guide to the background of Formula 1 has never been more important, and so when I was asked to write a brief introduction to *Grand Prix* I was delighted to do so, in the knowledge that this book will go a long way toward providing that guidance.

I sincerely hope you continue to enjoy the sport of grand prix racing – and that I may even be asked back next year to write another introduction as 1987 World Drivers' Champion!

THE FIRST EIGHTY YEARS

63

1906 AND ALL THAT

The origins of grand-prix racing lie in the Gordon Bennett Cup, an international race sponsored by an expatriate American newspaper magnate, in which each country could enter three cars of native manufacture. The first of these races was in 1900 and the last in 1905. By this time the French had become disenchanted with the entry limit: as the first great centre of the motor industry, France by now had many firms building racers, notably Panhard, Renault, Peugeot, Mors, Clément-Bayard, Darracq, De Diétrich, Gobron-Brillié, Richard-Brasier, and Turcat-Méry. They wanted an open, international race in which all marques could compete.

And so, for 1906, the Automobile Club de France (ACF) organised the first-ever Grand Prix (Great Prize). It killed the Gordon Bennett Cup stone dead. The race was over a 103.2km (63.9-mile) circuit of public roads east of Le Mans. It was run over two days, the cars doing six laps on each day – a total of 1238.4km (767.8 miles). The victor was Renault's chief test engineer, Ferenc Szisz, in a 13-litre, 90hp racer, averaging 101.2km/h (62.7 mph); second was the Italian Felice Nazzaro in a 16.3-litre, 100hp FIAT.

Preceding two pages *Some early Gordon Bennett races were run concurrently with major inter-city events. The last and most notorious of these was the 1903 Paris–Madrid race, which was stopped at Toulouse after several drivers and spectators had been killed in accidents. The best-known fatality was Marcel Renault (one of the car-making brothers) seen at the wheel of his 6.5-litre light racer a few minutes before it overturned at Couhé-Verac, south of Poitiers.*

Left *Winner Léon Théry in a Richard-Brasier leads the Hon. C.S. Rolls in a Wolseley in the last of the Gordon Bennett Cup races, run on a twisty circuit in the Auvergne (France) in 1905. He averaged 77.9km/h (48.3mph).*

Above *Two of the 13-litre Renault racers in the pit lane during the 1906 Grand Prix, run on a circuit of closed public roads a few miles east of Le Mans. The race was held on two of the hottest days of the decade and many drivers suffered eye injuries from flying grit and molten tar. The winning driver, Ferenc Szisz, had been Louis Renault's riding mechanic in the 1903 Paris–Madrid race.*

__Right__ Szisz speeds in his 13-litre, 90bhp Renault through La Ferté-Bernard on his way to victory in the 1906 Grand Prix.

__Below__ FIAT's Felice Nazzaro, who had come second in 1906, turned the tables on Szisz in the 1907 race near Dieppe. FIAT were pioneers in the use of overhead valves in racing cars.

RACING TOWARDS THE WAR

Through 1907-8 the Grand Prix de l'ACF established itself as the world's premier motor race, and during the years of weight limitations (*see below*) engine capacities of 18 litres and more became commonplace. Racing techniques developed, pit procedures improved, and many national racing colours were adopted.

In 1907 the Grand Prix was run over a 76.9km (47.7-mile) circuit near Dieppe, and this time Nazzaro's 4-cylinder, 16.3-litre FIAT, developing 130bhp, beat Szisz's 13-litre Renault by over six minutes. Worse (in French eyes) was to follow at Dieppe the following year, when Christian Laütenschlager, foreman-tester at Mercedes' factory, won in a 12.8-litre racer designed by Paul Daimler – and, moreover, German Benz cars came second and third.

Owing to a depression in the car industry, the next true Grand Prix did not take place until 1912, when it was again held at Dieppe. It was run concurrently with a race for *voiturettes* (3-litres maximum) sponsored by *L'Auto* magazine. The race was a triumph for a new French hero, Georges Boillot, driving the revolutionary new Peugeot L76 with its twin-overhead-camshaft, four-valves-per-cylinder engine of only 7.6 litres. Boillot won again at Amiens the following year.

Rules and Regulations: 1906-14

The ACF chopped and changed the regulations for its Grand Prix, taking account of developments in car and engine design. The main provisions for the six Grands Prix during this period were as follows:

1906 Weight limit of 1000kg (2200lb).

1907 Maximum fuel consumption permitted: 30 litres/100km (6.6gal/62 miles), equivalent to about $9\frac{1}{2}$ miles per gallon.

1908 Combined area of piston heads: $75cm^2$ (117 sq in), equivalent to a bore diameter of 155mm (6in) for 4-cylinder and 127mm (5in) for 6-cylinder engines.

1909–11 Grand Prix in abeyance owing to recession in French car industry.

1912 No weight or engine-capacity restrictions.

1913 Maximum fuel consumption permitted: 20 litres/100km (4.4gal/62 miles), equivalent to about 14 miles per gallon. Weight restricted to between 800 and 1100kg (1760 and 2420lb).

1914 Engine capacity $4\frac{1}{2}$ litres maximum; weight 1100kg (2420lb) maximum.

Felice Nazzaro (1881–1940)

Nazzaro, the greatest Italian driver of the period up to World War I, was apprenticed to the FIAT company at an early age, and was for some time employed as a chauffeur by Vincenzo Florio. He became a test engineer and then a racing driver for FIAT in the first years of this century, the company's formidable trio of drivers being made up by Vincenzo Lancia and Alessandro Cagno.

Nazzaro sprang to prominence in 1905 when he and Cagno took second and third places in the Gordon Bennett Cup in massive 75bhp FIATs; the following year he came second to Szisz in the first-ever Grand Prix. Nazzaro's greatest year, however, was 1907, when he won the three premier races of the season in three FIATs of quite different specification: the Targa Florio in the 7.4-litre 28-40hp '20-B' model; the Kaiserpreis (the German equivalent of a Grand Prix) in the 8-litre Taunus model; and the French Grand Prix with an F2, a massive 16.3-litre racer capable of 177km/h (110mph). His crowning achievement after World War I came in 1922 when, at the age of 41, he won the French Grand Prix at Strasbourg in a 2-litre Fiat Tipo 804. These cars were remarkably fast for their day and capacity, but efforts to reduce their weight had made them dangerously fragile. (Nazzaro's pleasure in his outstanding victory was soured by the death in this race of his nephew Biaggio, in a similar Fiat, who was thrown onto the track when his 804's rear axle snapped.) He retired from racing after his car broke down in the Italian Grand Prix of 1924, but he remained on Fiat's staff until shortly before his death in 1940.

Above *Poster for the 1912 Grand Prix – the first for four years – and the Coupe de* L'Auto *voiturette race run at the same meeting.*

Right *1912 Grand Prix: Georges Boillot on his way to victory in the advanced Peugeot L76. The race was run over two days, Boillot brilliantly nursing his car home after it lost two of its four gears on the second day. The Peugeot's triumph signalled the end of the slow-revving, mammoth-engined racers in grands prix.*

Georges Boillot (1885–1916)

During the Coupe de *L'Auto* of 1913, Georges Boillot was in the lead when, to the surprise of the Peugeot mechanics, he pulled into the pits, climbed out of his car and called for a glass of wine. Having unhurriedly quenched his thirst, he enquired casually as to how his rivals were doing, climbed back into his car, and drove to victory. The episode was characteristic of a man whose histrionic temperament, vanity and brilliance as a driver lent excitement to racing in the last few years before World War I and made him the idol of the French public.

Boillot made his name as a development engineer and driver of the bizarre Lion-Peugeot V-twin *voiturettes*. He and his team-mates Jules Goux (as good a driver as Boillot, though less flashy), and Paul Zuccarelli (formerly an engineer with Hispano-Suiza) all helped the brilliant Swiss engineer Ernest Henri in the design of the innovative Peugeot L76 and its successor developed for the 1914 Grand Prix (*see overleaf*).

At the outbreak of war he joined the French air force – one of the first pilots in a unit known as *Les Sportifs*. He died in May 1916 when, in a spirit typical of his performance on the racetrack, he took on seven German scouts singlehanded: the odds were hopeless and he was shot out of the sky.

***Above** Boillot also won the 1913 Grand Prix, which had reverted to a single-day event. His team-mate Jules Goux took another L76 to victory in the famous Indianapolis 500 that year, and they later joined forces to break a world record by covering more than 171km (106 miles) in one hour.*

***Left** Boillot first gained fame driving in* voiturette *races. Here he is on his way to winning the 1913 Coupe de* L'Auto *at Boulogne in a 3-litre Peugeot.*

THE 1914 GRAND PRIX

The French were vehemently chauvinistic in their attitude toward the Grand Prix: they regarded it as their race, and hated to see victory going to foreign cars. It is easy to imagine the emotional frenzy of the crowd at the 1914 Grand Prix (at Lyon), which was run only four weeks before the outbreak of World War I. It was, in fact, one of the most significant grands prix in history. Technically it proved to be a contest between what were then the two most advanced marques in the world – Peugeot of France and Mercedes of Germany. The 4.5-litre Peugeot engine, designed by Ernest Henri, can be regarded as the ancestor of the modern high-performance car engine: it used twin overhead camshafts to operate four valves per cylinder, and developed 112bhp at the then high speed of 2,900rpm. To improve cornering performance the Peugeots were fitted with brakes on all four wheels (the first time the system was used in the Grand Prix). Henri's opposite number in the Mercedes camp was Paul Daimler (son of the car pioneer). His cars also had engines of 4.5 litres (the maximum capacity permitted for this race), with single overhead camshafts, and four valves and three sparking plugs per cylinder; they developed 115bhp at 3,200rpm. Both cars used shaft drive rather than chains, developed power at more usable engine speeds than the vast, slow-revving cars of earlier days, and had far better handling.

The German team consisted of old hands

Right *Louis Wagner in his second-placed Mercedes on the back stretch of the 1914 Grand Prix circuit at Givors, south of Lyon. Though advanced in engine specification, the German cars had no front-wheel brakes, the foot-pedal operating a drum on the drive shaft while the outside hand-brake acted only on the rear wheels.*

Left *The winner, Christian Laütenschlager, on the steep, winding hill that culminated in the Piège de la Mort (Deathtrap) hairpin bend. He averaged 105.7km/h (65.7mph) for the race.*

Below *Boillot in his Peugeot. Its long tail, fitted specially for the race, increased the car's top speed.*

such as Laütenschlager, Otto Salzer and ex-Fiat driver Louis Wagner, and newcomer Max Sailer. Peugeot were led by Boillot and Jules Goux.

In spite of a legend to the contrary, the Germans had not planned a detailed race strategy; but Sailer's impetuosity served his team well. He went off like a rocket and was $1\frac{1}{2}$ minutes ahead of Boillot by the end of the third lap of the 37.5km (23.3-mile) circuit; on the fourth lap he broke the circuit record – and then one of his connecting rods snapped. He was out of the race, but his job was done: Boillot had already overstretched his car in a rash attempt to keep pace with Sailer. By now Laütenschlager in the second Mercedes was beginning to press Boillot, who immediately stepped up his speed. But the Mercedes challenge was remorseless: by lap 17 (with only three to go) Laüenschlager had cut Boillot's lead to 14 seconds, and on the 18th he passed him. By now the Peugeot was sick and on the next lap it threw a valve. And so it was that Laütenschlager, Wagner and Salzer recorded the first-ever 1–2–3 Grand Prix victory, Goux's Peugeot limping in in fourth place. The vast French crowd was stunned – and the official band found itself unable to play the German national anthem because it had 'mislaid' the music.

Right *The 1921 Grand Prix was run over the public-road circuit south of Le Mans that is now used for the 24-hour sportscar race. The picture shows the eight-cylinder Ballot driven by Louis Wagner (one of the Mercedes team in the 1914 race) into seventh place. The surface of the Le Mans circuit broke up during the race, which was described by one of the drivers of the winning Duesenberg team as 'a damn rock-hewing contest'.*

THE 1920s

The ACF held the first post-war Grand Prix in 1921 on a new public-road course, 17.26km (10.7 miles) long, at Le Mans – essentially the circuit still used today for the famous Le Mans 24-hour race. The Club adopted the 3-litre Indianapolis race formula – and the race appropriately went to the American Jimmy Murphy in his straight-eight Duesenberg.

In 1922 Italy held its own grand prix at newly opened Monza. Fiat straight-six Tipo 804s won not only this race but the French Grand Prix at Strasbourg. Sunbeam built virtually a replica of the Fiat and won the 1923 French GP at Tours and the Spanish Grand Prix at San Sebastian.

The finest racers of the later 1920s were built by Alfa Romeo, Bugatti and Delage. Sunbeam had 'borrowed' Fiat engineers to build their winning racer. Alfa Romeo sent Enzo Ferrari to lure the greatest Italian designer of all away from Fiat: Vittorio Jano, who produced the famous straight-eight P2, a quicker version of Fiat's superb 805. The P2, in the hands of Giuseppe Campari, won its first-ever grand prix (the French, at Lyon) in 1924, following it with the Italian and European (at Spa, Belgium), both going to Antonio Ascari.

Bugatti's most famous racer was the beautiful straight-eight Type 35 in its various forms, notably the 35C (1990cc, supercharged) and the 35B (2261cc, blown and unblown), both of these competing in the many free-formula races; there was also the Type 39 variant (1492cc, blown) to compete in the 1926-7 1½-litre GP formula.

But the dominant racer in the 1½-litre formula was the Delage. For 1926 the marque followed its fascinating, hugely complex 2-litre V12 racer with a superb 1½-litre straight-eight, the most innovative engine of its day, which in blown form developed a remarkable 170bhp. Its performance was initially hampered by heating problems, but for one glorious season (1927) ace driver Robert Benoist made mincemeat of the opposition. Then, for 1928, the *formula libre* (unlimited engine-capacity) was introduced.

Below *Ettore Bugatti's masterpiece, the Type 35, first raced in the French Grand Prix of 1924. More than 200 in various forms were built over the next seven years. The Type 35B with supercharger was introduced in 1927; the beautifully maintained example shown here still competes regularly in Vintage races and is capable of more than 205km/h (130mph).*

Left *Vittorio Jano stands in front of his first car for Alfa Romeo, the P2 grand-prix racer closely modelled on the Fiat 805 that he had helped to design. The P2 had three major triumphs in 1924.*

Rules and Regulations: 1921–33

1921 Minimum weight 800kg (1760lb); engine capacity 3 litres maximum.
1922–4 Minimum weight 650kg (1430lb); engine capacity 2 litres maximum.
1925 As above; riding mechanics banned but two-seat body still required; rear-view mirrors obligatory.
1926 Minimum weight 600kg (1320lb); engine capacity $1\frac{1}{2}$ litres maximum; single-seat body style allowed.
1927 Minimum weight 700kg (1540lb); engine capacity $1\frac{1}{2}$ litres maximum.
1928 Engine capacity: no limit; minimum weight 550–750kg (1210–1650lb), depending on engine size; race distance 600km (372 miles) minimum.
1929 Commercial petrol mandatory, with consumption limit of about 14.5 miles per gallon.
1930 As above, with option of adding 30 per cent benzole to commercial fuel.
1931 *Formula libre* (free formula); race duration 10 hours minimum.
1932 *Formula libre*; race duration 5–10 hours.
1933 *Formula libre*; race distance 500km (310 miles) minimum.

Below *Jano's greatest grand-prix car, the Alfa Romeo Tipo B (or P3), won practically everything in sight in seasons 1932-3. Light in weight, supremely agile, and handsome in appearance, the Tipo B's further development ceased with Alfa Romeo's near bankruptcy at the end of 1932.*

FREE FORMULA

The *formula libre*, which in various guises was to last until the end of the 1933 season, saw the departure of the Delage, Sunbeam and bankrupt Talbot from the grand-prix scene. At the end of the decade a new Italian marque, Maserati, made an impressive entrance, and in 1930 its powerful 2½-litre supercharged straight-eight gained five grand-prix victories. Ettore Bugatti responded with the twin-cam Type 51, powered by a supercharged straight-eight engine of 2 or 2.3 litres based on an American Miller design, and followed this with the powerful but tricky 4.9-litre Type 54.

Then, in 1932, came one of the most revered of all grand-prix racers: Vittorio Jano's masterpiece, the Alfa Romeo Tipo B, commonly known as the P3 – the first purpose-built *monoposto* (single-seat) GP car. The P3's supercharged straight-eight engine was originally of 2654cc and developed 215bhp. In the 1932 season it won all but two of the races it entered; in many events the Alfa works team, run by the young Enzo Ferrari, filled second and third spots as well. More powerful versions were developed over the next three seasons. And in the 1935 German Grand Prix the car achieved its apotheosis: a 3.8-litre version, driven with unparalleled brilliance by Tazio Nuvolari on a rain-soaked Nürburgring, humbled all nine of the supposedly unbeatable Mercedes-Benz and Auto Union racers developing at least 100bhp more than the Alfa.

Tazio Nuvolari (1892–1953)

'The Flying Mantuan' is still regarded by many as the greatest racing driver of all. At the height of his fame in the 1930s he was known simply but unequivocally as Il Maestro (The Master), and in Italy he was a national hero. On the racetrack his short, slight figure, clothed in a yellow turtle-neck sweater, sky-blue trousers, and brown shoes with yellow laces, was instantly recognisable. At the wheel, his extraordinary facial contortions belied the cool, unspectacular economy of his driving style. He was probably the inventor of the technique of fast cornering known as the four-wheel drift.

For most of the 1930s Nuvolari drove Alfa Romeos (and sometimes Maseratis), which from 1934 onwards were outclassed in specification and performance by the new Mercedes-Benz and Auto Union racers. An idea of Nuvolari's genius can be seen in the fact that in 1934–6 he won 14 grands prix and was placed in nine others, while the great Rudolf Caracciola, the number one driver of the Mercedes-Benz team, won nine and was placed in four. If his most famous victory was in the 1935 German Grand Prixs an almost equally startling demonstration of his skill came in the 1934 Monza Grand Prix. In order to lighten his Maserati for the weigh-in before the race, his crew drained the hydraulic fluid from the brake system – and then forgot to put it back! In spite of having virtually no brakes, Nuvolari came in fifth.

His courage was legendary. In 1934, with his right leg encased in plaster seven weeks after he had broken it in a crash at Alessandria, he entered for the Avus Grand Prix on the circuit near Berlin. Although he had only one usable foot to actuate the accelerator, clutch, and brake pedals, he took fourth place. He broke ribs so often that he had a special 'corset' of bandages made for him so that he could race while the fractures were mending.

Nuvolari was strenuously wooed by the managers of the Mercedes and Auto Union teams, and eventually he joined Auto Union in 1938, finishing fourth in his first race and winning the Italian and Donington grands prix that season.

His career in major sports-car races was concentrated mainly in the years 1930–5. During that period he won the Mille Miglia twice (1930, 1933) and was second once (1934); he won the Targa Florio twice (1931, 1932), the Le Mans 24-hours once (1933), and the RAC Tourist Trophy race twice (1930, 1933).

Above *Tazio Nuvolari in his 1930s heyday. He was a motor-cycling champion before he became the greatest grand-prix and sportscar driver of the years before World War II.*

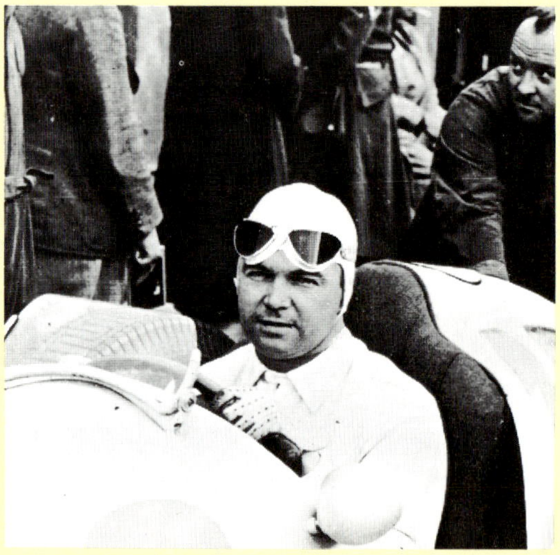

Rudolf Caracciola (1901–59)

In spite of his dark hair and Italian-sounding surname, Rudolf Caracciola was a German born in the Rhineland, the son of a hotelier of Remagen. He worked during the early 1920s for the Fafnir motor factory and drove the firm's 1.9-litre Type 471 sports car in his first race, at the Avus circuit, in 1922. His talent was soon spotted by Mercedes and he began his long career with the great Stuttgart firm in 1924, at first taking part mainly in hill-climb and sprint races. He was entered in the first-ever German Grand Prix, at the Avus in 1926, and leapt into immediate international prominence by winning the race, driving the ill-handling 2-litre Mercedes brilliantly on the rain-soaked track. Caracciola's skill in the wet was unrivalled in his day – he was known as Regenmeister (Rainmaster) and was unmatched in grand-prix racing until Stirling Moss reached his peak in the 1950s.

Caracciola proved himself one of the great grand-prix drivers in the 1935–9 seasons. There is no doubt that the Mercedes-Benz and, to a lesser extent, the Auto Unions of that period were greatly in advance of anything the Italians or the French manufacturers could put against them. But equally the cars needed drivers of outstanding skill to get the best out of them. Caracciola proved unquestionably the greatest of the team of Mercedes drivers of that era, winning 14 grands prix (including the German race five times) in the last six seasons before World War II.

Like other Mercedes and Auto Union drivers, Caracciola also competed in major hill-climb events in the 1930s. Although not so great in this field as 'Bergmeister' Hans Stuck, he broke the record for the notorious Klausen hill-climb in 1934 in a Mercedes W25.

GERMANY TRIUMPHANT

In 1933 the Nazi government in Germany began to subsidize the development of not one but two world-beating grand-prix teams: the well-established Mercedes-Benz stable and the newly emergent Auto Union, which was to build racers designed by Dr Ferdinand Porsche. That year the Association Internationale des Automobile Clubs Reconnus (AIACR), the grand-prix ruling body, announced that for 1934 the new formula would have a *maximum* weight limit of 750kg (1650lb), excluding fuel, oil, water and tyres.

For Mercedes, designer Hans Nibel's team produced the W25, powered by an advanced twin-cam straight-eight of 3360cc and with all-independent suspension. Porsche came up with

his sensational mid-engined V16 racer, with limited-slip differential but somewhat tail-happy handling. In 1935–7 both marques steadily developed and improved their racers (the Mercedes culminating in the awesome W125, which was getting 646bhp from its 5.66-litre engine). For 1938–9 the formula was changed to a *minimum* weight of 800kg (1760lb) and a maximum engine capacity of 3 litres supercharged and 4½ litres unsupercharged. The superb Mercedes W154 and its 1939 refinement, the W163 – a true masterpiece of engineering, its four-cam V12 engine producing 484bhp with two-stage supercharging – were matched by the equally powerful Auto Union D-Type.

From 1935 until the outbreak of World War II the German teams were not merely dominant but, collectively, virtually invincible. Allied to the astonishing power, sophistication and increasing reliability of their cars was the ruthlessly efficient organization of their works teams, and the Mercedes team manager, the rotund Alfred Neubauer, with his battered trilby and necklace of stopwatches, became an ominously familiar figure to rival teams all over Europe.

Alfa Romeo gave up the grand-prix battle, concentrating on *voiturette* racing and on the sports-car events they came to dominate with a series of brilliant Jano-designed cars. In 1938 Delahaye and Talbot briefly entered the lists with sadly inferior 4½-litre unblown racers. Maserati, with their handsome, very fast but unreliable 8CTF 3-litre supercharged racer produced on a shoestring, occasionally gave the Germans a scare (but the car's only real success came when it went to America and won the Indianapolis 500 race two years running). The period closed in September 1939 when Nuvolari, lured to Auto Union the year before, won the Yugoslav Grand Prix on the day war was declared.

Above *Caracciola in the Mercedes-Benz W154, in which he won the drivers' championship for the third year running in 1938. The V12 car was developed for the 3-litre formula introduced that year, and won six major races in five countries. Like the rival Auto Union D-type it used limited-slip differential, a refinement available on popular road cars only in the 1980s.*

Agip
Agip
Agip
Agip
Agip
Agip
RISTORANTE
FERODO

THE WORLD CHAMPIONSHIPS

For 1948 the sport's new governing body, the Fédération Internationale de l'Automobile (FIA), specified a grand-prix formula ($1\frac{1}{2}$ litres blown, $4\frac{1}{2}$ litres unblown) to suit existing (essentially pre-war) machinery. Best of the unblown cars were the Lago-Talbots; but the year belonged to the supercharged Alfa Romeo Tipo 158 Alfetta, which had been designed by Jano's chief aide, Gioacchino Colombo, in 1938. Alfa withdrew from racing in 1949 following the deaths of their three leading drivers – Jean-Pierre Wimille and the great veteran Achille Varzi in crashes and Count Carlo Trossi from cancer – and the season was dominated by a new *équipe*, Ferrari, and its rising star Alberto Ascari.

In 1950 the FIA launched two World Championships – one for constructors, the other for drivers. The formula was unchanged and the improved Alfetta, Tipo 159, triumphed in the first two years, Dr 'Nino' Farina taking the drivers' title in 1950 and Juan Manuel Fangio in 1951. Alfa Romeo then retired from racing.

For 1952–3 the FIA changed the specification to Formula B (or Formula 2 as it came to be called) – a *voiturette* class for unblown 2-litre cars. Ferrari was totally in charge in these two seasons, its four-cylinder Tipo 500 F2s winning 14 consecutive GPs.

***Left** The Alfa Romeo Tipo 158, designed by Gioacchino Colombo (who later found fame with Ferrari), was originally intended for* voiturette *racing. The car dominated the grand-prix scene in 1948, was withdrawn in 1949, then won the new world championship in 1950 and 1951. Of its total of 33 grand-prix victories, 26 came in succession. By 1951 its final form (Tipo 159) was getting an astonishing 420bhp from its $1\frac{1}{2}$-litre engine and could manage barely 2mpg on its alcohol fuel. The picture shows a Tipo 158 on the starting line at the famous Monza circuit.*

Right A view into the engine compartment of the Ferrari 500 F2 which Alberto Ascari drove to victory in the 1953 British Grand Prix. Relatively small and simple by Ferrari standards, the four-cylinder unsupercharged engine developed 180bhp at 7,500rpm; its two twin-choke Weber carburettors are in the foreground. The 500 F2 won 30 out of its 33 races in two years.

Alberto Ascari (1918–55)

'Ciccio' Ascari, son of the great Alfa driver of the early 1920s, gained early racing experience on motorcycles, and had his first big motorcar race in 1940, when Enzo Ferrari offered him a drive in his first model, the Fiat-based Vettura 815, in the Mille Miglia. After the war he drove Cisitalias and works Maseratis for a few seasons. In 1949 Ascari and his mentor, Luigi Villoresi, joined Ferrari, Ascari winning the Italian and Swiss grands prix in Tipo 166s. Ascari's two greatest seasons were 1952 and 1953. The formula (2-litre, unsupercharged) was unexciting, but Ferrari's new chief designer, Aurelio Lampredi had come up with a car perfectly suited to its job, the Tipo 500 F2. Of the 14 consecutive grands prix won by Ferrari in those two seasons, Ascari took 11 and in both years ran away with the drivers' title by huge margins.

In 1954 Ascari was lured away to Lancia, then preparing its Jano-designed D50 V8s for the new $2\frac{1}{2}$-litre formula. The following season the cars finally got onto the circuits, proving immensely fast, though difficult to handle. In the Monaco Grand Prix Ascari, leading on the 80th lap, came out of the tunnel, braked to negotiate the water-front chicane, locked one of his front wheels – and the car plunged into the harbour. Amazingly, Ascari escaped with bruises. Four days later he took a Ferrari sportscar to Monza to test his nerve. On his third lap the car struck the edge of the track and rolled over, Ascari dying soon afterwards. Like his father, he was killed at the age of 36 on the 26th day of the month.

Juan Manuel Fangio (born 1911)

Stirling Moss, number two to Fangio in the Mercedes team in 1955, regarded 'El Chueco' (Bandylegs) as the greatest grand-prix driver he had ever seen. Post-war, certainly, his record is incomparable: although Jim Clark, Jackie Stewart and Alain Prost all won more grands prix, none of them approached his astonishing wins-to-races ratio of 24 victories in 51 starts – all achieved, moreover, in a championship career that did not begin until he was 38 years old!

He learnt his trade in his native Argentina in the 1930s, driving in long-distance road races. His first experience in true racing cars was in 1948 when, after demonstrating his talent in a series of events in Buenos Aires, he was brought to Europe by Jean-Pierre Wimille to race Simcas. He won his first race (the San Remo Grand Prix). He was invited to join the Alfa Romeo works team for 1950, when he won three GPs and was runner-up in the championship; the following year he took the title.

His second and third titles came in 1954 and 1955 with Mercedes; the following year, the Germans having withdrawn from racing, he moved to Ferrari and took his fourth title. His fifth (and fourth in a row) was with Maserati. He retired in 1958.

Fangio's success was based on immaculate technique, a fine tactical sense, patience, and an unmatched ability to nurse ailing cars to victory. That he could also drive with unparalleled ferocity he showed in the title-clinching German Grand Prix of 1957, when he broke the lap record five times in the first 11 laps in his ageing Maserati 250F; lost over a minute in a disastrous refuelling stop; and finally destroyed the challenges of Hawthorn and Collins in the very fast Lancia-Ferraris on the 20th lap, when he sliced a further six seconds off an already astonishing lap record.

THE MERCS RETURN

For 1954 the FIA specified a 750cc blown/2½ litres unblown formula. Ferrari, Maserati and newcomers Lancia were joined, halfway through the season, by Mercedes-Benz, re-entering the grand-prix circus after 15 years; all of these marques opted for unblown engines. The German fuel-injected, straight-eight W196 racers, with novel space-frame chassis and aerodynamic bodywork, won the first GP they contested (the French at Reims) and dominated the rest of the season. Juan Manuel Fangio took the drivers' title, after starting the season with Maserati but then accepting a lucrative Mercedes offer. In 1955 the W196 was virtually unbeatable and Fangio took his third title. But Mercedes withdrew from all racing at the end of that season after one of their sportsracing 300SLR cars, 3-litre derivatives of the grand-prix car, had crashed at Le Mans, killing 89 people.

Left *Stirling Moss (6) and Juan Manuel Fangio (2) head the field in their Mercedes W196s in the 1955 Monaco Grand Prix; neither finished the race. The W196 was available with two variations of bodywork; the other had an all-enveloping streamlined body that gave it a higher top speed but was hard to manoeuvre accurately on twisty circuits.*

Right *Alfred Neubauer was team manager of the victorious Mercedes grand-prix teams both in the 1930s and in the 1954–5 seasons.*

Below *Stirling Moss aboard one of his favourite cars, the Maserati 250F, on his way to victory in the 1956 Monaco Grand Prix, which he led from start to finish. The 250F, partly designed by Colombo, was one of those cars in which the whole is much better than its fairly conventional parts might suggest. In four seasons, 1954–7, it won 22 Formula 1 races, including seven in 1957 when it took Fangio to his fifth and final drivers' title.*

BRITISH BREAKTHROUGH

The last grand prix of the 1955 season, at Syracuse (Sicily), saw the Maserati team humbled by Tony Brooks' Connaught – the first all-British victory in a European GP since Henry Segrave's Sunbeam had won at San Sebastian in 1924.

The British were encouraged. And in 1956, while Fangio won his fourth title (in the very fast Jano-designed Lancia D50 V8, racing in Ferrari colours after the Lancia family sold their car interests to an industrial consortium), the aerodynamically advanced, 2½-litre, 4-cylinder Vanwall became competitive.

The following year, although thwarted again by Fangio winning his fifth and last title (with Maserati), Vanwalls in the hands of Stirling Moss, Brooks and Stuart Lewis-Evans began taking the chequered flag. In 1958 the British team fought a furious, season-long battle with the Ferrari Dino 246s driven by Mike Hawthorn and Peter Collins. Going into the final race, at Casablanca, the drivers' title lay between Moss and Hawthorn. By coming second Hawthorn clinched the title by a single point; but winner Moss had the satisfaction of securing the first-ever British constructors' title for Vanwall.

Left *Stirling Moss, with cups and victor's laurels after winning the 1957 Italian Grand Prix for Vanwall.*

Stirling Moss (born 1929)

Moss never won the drivers' title – he was runner-up four years running (1955–8) – but he was the greatest all-rounder since Nuvolari, excelling equally as a grand-prix, sportscar and rally driver. His first qualifying GP was the Swiss at Berne in 1951. In 1954 he bought a Maserati 250F, took third place in his first race, and was invited to join Maserati's works team. In that year's Italian GP at Monza he outdrove the W196s of Fangio and Hermann Lang until, with only 10 laps to go, his fuel tank sprang a leak. But this drive was enough to secure him a place in the Mercedes team for 1955, when he won the British GP. With Mercedes' withdrawal from racing, Moss rejoined Maserati for 1956 and won the Monaco and Italian GPs as well as many non-qualifying events. For 1957–8 he spearheaded Vanwall's campaigns, and also achieved one of his greatest victories, in the Argentine GP, in a prototype mid-engined Cooper.

For 1960 Moss drove the fast but fragile new Lotus 18, winning at Monaco but then suffering two broken legs when his car lost a rear wheel in practice for the Belgian GP – but he went on to win the U.S. GP later in the season. For 1961, still with the now outdated Lotus 18, he won the Monaco and German GPs against all odds. His racing career ended in 1962 when he suffered serious head injuries when crashing, inexplicably, in a race at the Goodwood Easter meeting.

THE MID-ENGINE TAKEOVER

The year 1958 was the end of the line for the classic front-engined grand-prix car. At their Surbiton (Surrey) garage the Cooper car company had launched a Formula 2 version of their hugely successful mid-engined, all-independently-sprung F3 racer. The new car, using a 1½-litre Coventry Climax engine descended from a fire pump, proved competitive. In January 1958, with a 2-litre Climax engine, the car was entered for the Argentine GP. The organisers at first thought the car was a toy – but Stirling Moss drove the Cooper to a stunning victory, at record speed, over the Ferrari and Maserati teams.

For 1959 a full 2½-litre Climax engine was ready and the Coopers put the other works teams to the sword, winning five GPs, taking the constructors' championship and giving Jack Brabham his first drivers' title. The following year – with BRM, Lotus and even Ferrari also fielding mid-engined cars – Cooper and Brabham took their titles even more decisively, winning six of the qualifying races.

Amid controversy (and bitterness among British interests) a 1½-litre formula had been declared for 1961. Ferrari had a potent mid-engined version of the V6 Dino 246, and it proved superior to the old F2 designs to which the shoestring Cooper outfit was obliged to revert. The Dino 156 F1, as the new model was designated, was instantly recognizable by its two air-intake nostrils at the front; it gave Ferrari the constructors' title and American Phil Hill the drivers', after his closest challenger, team-mate Wolfgang von Trips, was killed in the deciding race, the Italian GP at Monza.

Below left Tony Brooks in the Vanwall which he and Stirling Moss drove to victory in the 1957 Grand Prix at Aintree. The car's low-drag body brought new aero-dynamic standards to F1 racing.

Below Phil Hill at Loew's hairpin in the 1961 Monaco Grand Prix in Ferrari's first rear-engined F1 car, the 156 F1, based on the front-engined 256 F1 of 1958. Third at Monaco, Hill took the 1961 drivers' title.

Right Stirling Moss, the winner, in the rear-engined Lotus Climax, leads Richie Ginther (Ferrari 156 F1) around Loew's in the 1961 Monaco GP. Lotus were second that year to Ferrari in the constructors' championship.

NLOP DUN

Rules and Regulations: 1954–65

Grand-prix and formula racing underwent considerable change during this period of 12 years. The international single-seater formulas adopted were as follows:

1954–7 Capacity limit of $2\frac{1}{2}$ litres unsupercharged or 750 cc supercharged, weight optional. Races to last minimum 3 hours or 500 km (312 miles). Formula 2 suspended.

1958–60 Capacity restrictions as above; racing fuels barred, use of 100–30-octane aviation-grade 'AvGas' compulsory. Race distance cut to 300 km (180 miles) or minimum 2 hours. New unsupercharged $1\frac{1}{2}$-litre Formula 2 introduced.

1959 Production-based single-seater Formula Junior introduced: 1,100 cc push-rod engines, weight minimums 360 kg (790 lb) with 1-litre engine or 400 kg (880 lb) with 1,100 cc.

1961–5 New $1\frac{1}{2}$-litre unsupercharged Formula 1; commercial fuel. Minimum weight 450 kg (990 lb). Enveloping bodies banned. Onboard starters and roll-over driver-protection obligatory. Formula 2 suspended; Formula Junior continued until 1963.

1964–6 New 1-litre Formulas 2 and 3 introduced, replacing Junior. F2 allowed free-design racing engines while F3 allowed only production-based push-rod units.

Below *Jim Clark on his way to victory in the 1962 British Grand Prix at Aintree – one of his five wins that year which made him runner-up for the drivers' title. His car was the brilliant Lotus 25 monocoque racer which, in its fuel-injected form, took the title in 1963.*

Right *Clark after completing a victory lap following the non-qualifying 1964 British European Auto Racing Grand Prix at Brands Hatch in a Lotus Climax. At right is Lotus chief Colin Chapman.*

Jim Clark (1937–68)

Considered by many to have been the greatest British grand-prix driver of all, Clark began racing in local sprints and sportscar events in the 1950s. His grand-prix career was launched in 1961 when he became top driver for Lotus. His immense talent and his affinity for Colin Chapman's cars became sensationally apparent in December that year when he won the South African, the Natal and the Rand grands prix in the space of 17 days. In 1962 Graham Hill beat him to the title by a whisker after Clark had won the Belgian, British, United States and Mexican grands prix. But the following year Clark was virtually unbeatable in the wonderful Lotus 25: he scored a record seven *grande-épreuve* victories and had clinched the title with three events still to be run! He also took second place in the gruelling Indianapolis 500 race in a mid-engined Lotus-Ford which old hands at the famous 'Brickyard' had dismissed as a toy racer. In 1965 he took the title again – and at Indianapolis he became the first European driver to win the 500 for 45 years, leading for all but 10 of the 200 laps.

For 1966, the first year of the 3-litre formula, Clark had to make do with the 2-litre Lotus while the team's 3-litre units were being prepared. By 1968 Chapman had got the bugs out of what would prove to be an all-conquering car, the Ford-Cosworth DFV-powered Lotus 49, and a seemingly inevitable third title awaited Clark. In April that year, however, in a Formula 2 race at Hockenheim, West Germany, his car skidded off the circuit for still-unexplained reasons, and crashed broadside into a tree. Clark died in hospital shortly afterwards. Of the 72 grands prix he entered, Clark won 25 – better than one in three.

Graham Hill (1929–75)

After working as a driver-mechanic for several seasons Hill became a full-time driver for Lotus in 1958, but lack of success in the notoriously fragile Lotus 16s led to his joining the crisis-torn BRM team the following year. He remained faithful to BRM for six seasons, his patience being rewarded by BRM's only championship, and Hill's first world title, in 1962. For the next three years he was runner-up for the drivers' title, his great rival during this period being Jim Clark. In 1966 Hill won bravely, if somewhat fortuitously, the Indianapolis 500 race (and a considerable fortune) in a Lola-Ford.

The following year he teamed up with Clark to drive the Lotus 49s. Hill had an indifferent season, but in 1968 the car's reliability was transformed and Hill went on to take the drivers' title in the last grand prix of the season. The year 1969 saw him win the Monaco Grand Prix for a record fifth time, but a terrible accident, due to a faulty tyre, almost cost him his life in the United States Grand Prix at Watkins Glen. His legs were badly injured and he never regained his form as a grand-prix driver.

From 1973 onwards he raced his own Cosworth-powered Shadow and Lola grand-prix cars, in 1975 employing Alan Jones and Tony Brise as his top drivers and doing little racing himself. In November of that year, when returning from testing a new car on the Paul Ricard circuit in the south of France, the aircraft Hill was piloting crashed on the northern outskirts of London; Hill, Tony Brise, the team manager, the team designer, and two others were killed.

Left *Graham Hill on 'home' ground – the twisting streets of Monte Carlo, where he won the Monaco Grand Prix five times in seven years (1963–9), coming second and third in the other two years. The picture shows him winning his first Monaco in 1963, driving the BRM with which he had captured the first of his two drivers' titles the previous season.*

ENTER THE MONOCOQUE RACER

The years from 1962 to 1965 (after which the formula changed) saw a series of running battles between Lotus and BRM, with interventions by Ferrari. An all-British outfit, BRM (British Racing Motors), whose leading figures were veteran racing driver Raymond Mays and designer Peter Berthon, had to wait nine years for their first grand-prix victory (the 1959 Dutch race) and another three for their second (the 1962 Dutch); but the latter victory at last opened the floodgates – a total of 11 wins in four seasons. In 1962 the season-long struggle between Graham Hill (BRM) and Jim Clark (Lotus) ended in Hill's favour with his fourth GP win of the season in the South African race. BRM, like Ferrari, designed and built their own engines, transmission, chassis and body; their jewel-like V8 engine, with transistorised ignition and fuel injection, could turn at a (then) astonishing 12,000 rpm.

In 1963 the tables were turned decisively by the Lotus 25, which now added reliability to the superb handling inherent in Colin Chapman's innovative monocoque (chassisless) design, in which the car's structural strength derived from the body-shell components. Clark simply ran away with the championship, clinching the drivers' and constructors' titles while there were still three GPs to run. In the close-run 1964 campaign, Clark had three more victories; but now it was Ferrari's turn. Their updated Dino 156 F1 Aero V8 with semi-monocoque body won the constructors' title and driver John Surtees (an ex-motorcycling champion) took the drivers' title by one point from Graham Hill. Finally, in the last season of the $1\frac{1}{2}$-litre formula, Clark came good again in 1965. The Lotus 25 had given way to the 33, basically similar but with a 32-valve Climax engine, which he drove to six grand-prix victories. By then, such was Chapman's prestige that all the truly competitive works teams were driving cars of monocoque construction.

Jack Brabham (born 1926)

'Black Jack' Brabham arrived in Britain in 1955, having gained experience driving a Cooper-Bristol in his native New South Wales and New Zealand, and that year made his debut in the British Grand Prix at Aintree in a mid-engined Cooper. During the next three seasons he drove almost exclusively for Cooper, taking the Formula 2 title in 1958.

In 1959 Cooper entered its Climax-engined $2\frac{1}{2}$-litre cars in Formula 1 events, winning the championship from Ferrari by a whisker, and Brabham took the drivers' title. The following year he retained his title by winning five grands prix in succession.

The Coopers proved uncompetitive in the 1961 season with the new $1\frac{1}{2}$-litre formula. Brabham now decided to branch out on his own as both driver and constructor, for 1963 signing American Dan Gurney as second driver. The new *équipe* won its first GP (the French) the following year.

In 1966 the hurriedly introduced 3-litre formula caught most of the constructors napping – except for Brabham, who soon had an Australian Repco engine in highly competitive trim. He won four GPs that year, becoming the first driver in history to take the constructors' title in a car of his own design. In the following year, New Zealander Denny Hulme took the drivers' title and clinched the constructors' for Repco-Brabham, while Brabham was runner-up for drivers' honours.

__Below__ Jack Brabham winning the 1966 British Grand Prix at Brands Hatch in his Repco-Brabham, instantly recognisable by its writhing tangle of exhaust pipes. Brabham was the only team to have a truly race-ready engine for the new 3-litre formula in 1966, the Australian Repco company supplying him with a V8 unit based on a General Motors design (another version of which was used in the Rover V8 road car of the early 1970s).

THE CIRCUS EXPANDS

Whereas it had been common for the Formula 1 field of the 1950s to comprise perhaps a dozen cars, setting off on a 500km (312-mile) grand prix, the 3-litre era could see as many as 35 cars attempting to qualify for up to 32 grid places in a race of only 250 km (155 miles) or some 90 minutes' duration. This recipe as packaged and sold in the countries of Europe, North America, South America, South Africa and Japan, proved very successful, though many die-hard enthusiasts decried the passing of what they saw as 'proper' grand-prix racing. Today the races vary in length from 253.5 km (157.5 miles) at Detroit to 315.5 km (196.1 miles) at Brands Hatch; and the circuits vary from 3.3 km (2.1 miles) in length at Monaco to 6.9 km (4.3 miles) at Spa-Francorchamps (Belgium). From there being nine World Championship races in 1966, the first year of the new formula, the class developed to support no fewer than 17 by 1977. That figure is much the same today, though some of the countries staging the races have changed.

Rules and Regulations: 1966–86

For 1966 the FIA's sporting body, the Commission Sportive Internationale (CSI), introduced the 3-litre unblown/1½-litre supercharged formula. Jack Brabham's cars triumphed for the first two years. Thereafter, and for more than a decade, Formula 1 was to be dominated by the Ford-Cosworth DFV V8 engine, used exclusively by Lotus in 1967 and subsequently by a number of teams; it remained virtually unchallenged, except by Ferrari flat-12 power units in the Lauda years (1975–7), until Renault's turbocharged 1½-litre engine achieved reliability at the close of the 1970s.

Above *Jackie Stewart in the Ken Tyrrell Matra-Ford MS80 during practice for the 1969 Monaco Grand Prix. The high wings mounted over the rear wheels on the Matra (and on the Lotus-Ford behind it) were banned from the race proper. Stewart retired with a broken drive shaft after leading the race, but went on to take the first of his three drivers' titles that year.*

Jackie Stewart (born 1939)

Stewart's serious entry to motor racing came in 1963 after Ken Tyrrell had offered him a test drive in a Formula 3 Cooper-BMC at Goodwood. His rise through Formula 3 and Formula 2 was sensational. In 1964 he won all but two of the Formula 3 races he entered; finished second in his very first Formula 2 race; and in December, while deputising for Jim Clark, he won the second heat of the Formula 1 Rand Grand Prix in South Africa. He instantly became the hottest property among the grand prix rookies, and joined BRM as second driver to Graham Hill for the 1965 season. He won the Italian Grand Prix, was second in the Belgian and Dutch, third at Monaco – and took third place in the drivers' championship behind Clark and Hill.

What promised to be a meteoric rise to the top was interrupted in 1966 when, on a rain-flooded Spa circuit in the Belgian Grand Prix, Stewart's BRM spun off the track. He was rescued by Graham Hill – whose BRM had also crashed – who helped to cut him free from the wrecked car. Stewart had a broken shoulder and a cracked rib.

For 1968, with the BRM in decline, Stewart joined Ken Tyrrell (for whom he had continued to race Formula 2 cars in 1965–7). Tyrrell was now fitting his Matra cars with the Cosworth V8 engine hitherto available only to Lotus. In this first season the Matra-Ford proved fast but not always reliable; Stewart, in addition, broke his wrist in a Formula 2 race at Jarama (Spain) and had to miss a couple of championship-qualifying races. But he won the Dutch Grand Prix at Zandvoort, and followed this by one of his supreme performances, winning the German Grand Prix at the rain- and fog-blanketed Nürburgring by the almost ridiculous margin of four minutes.

The following year the Matra-Ford was almost invincible, Stewart taking the title with six victories. For 1970 Tyrrell used March chassis (Matra requiring theirs for a new V12 engine of their own design) and Stewart won only a single grand prix, the title going to Jochen Rindt (Lotus) with Jacky Ickx (Ferrari) coming second. But in 1971, after early-season failures, Stewart clinched his second title with victories in the Spanish, Monaco, French, British, German, and Canadian grands prix – his win on the tortuous Monaco circuit being achieved without benefit of rear-wheel brakes! After Brazilian Emerson Fittipaldi had taken his first title in 1972, Stewart's third and last title came in 1973 – his fourth place at Monza, after a supremely determined effort following a lengthy pit stop, giving him enough points to frustrate Emerson Fittipaldi's challenge for Lotus.

Stewart's total of 27 *grandes épreuves* (out of 99 starts) was not equalled until Alain Prost won the 1987 Belgian Grand Prix. Like Fangio and Clark before him (and like Niki Lauda in 1975–7) he dominated most of the races he entered so long as his car was up to scratch. Stewart was an heir to the Jack Brabham tradition of technologist drivers. He spent countless hours testing the suspension systems and tyres of his cars and contributed significantly to the art of 'setting-up' racers.

Below *The Ford-Cosworth V8 3-litre engine was the most successful and widely used power unit in the history of Formula 1 racing: its first victory (in its first grand prix) was at the 1967 Dutch GP, when it powered Jim Clark's Lotus 49; its 155th and last victory was in Michele Alboreto's Tyrrell Ford in the Detroit GP of 1983.*

Above James Hunt driving his McLaren-Ford to third place in the Japanese GP, the last race of the season, to secure the 1976 drivers' title. Niki Lauda – who finished one point behind Hunt in the championship – had retired after the second lap, judging rain-lashed Mount Fuji circuit to be unsafe. The race was won by Mario Andretti (Lotus-Ford) from Patrick Depailler (Tyrrell-Ford).

Following two pages Niki Lauda in Casino Square in the Monaco Grand Prix of 1977. He came second to Jody Scheckter, but he went on to take his second world title for Ferrari, in the 312 T2.

THE TURBO REVOLUTION

By the mid-1970s most of the Formula 1 teams – and all the more successful ones except for Ferrari – were using the Cosworth DFV V8 engine. Producing about 410bhp in the 1967 season, the unit was progressively improved until by 1972–4, when Emerson Fittipaldi won two titles and came second to Jackie Stewart in the other, it was pushing out about 480bhp. The Niki Lauda years (*see overleaf*) were interrupted in 1976 by James Hunt, driving for the immensely efficient McLaren team.

Then, in 1977, Renault re-entered the grand-prix scene, bringing with them a 1½-litre turbo-charged V6 engine. Their turbo engine proved extremely fast (and prodigiously thirsty); but it lacked the Cosworth's by now impeccable reliability, and at first the cars lost ground to their more conventional rivals when accelerating out of corners because there was a slight pause ('turbo-lag') before the extra power conferred by the turbo unit took effect. But clearly turbo-charged engines, promising far greater power than normally aspirated ones of twice the capacity, were the Formula 1 power units of the future. (Renault were soon to retire from the Formula 1 scene – but not until they had won the 1979 French Grand Prix, the marque's first victory since Ferenc Szisz's historic triumph 73 years before.)

Tyres were another area of fierce competition. A tyre war between Dunlop, Firestone and Goodyear, which started in 1964, had flared anew in the early years of the 3-litre formula. Dunlop gave up after 1970, as did Firestone at the end of 1974, leaving Goodyear with a monopoly that lasted until Michelin entered the fray in 1978.

Right *Renault re-entered grand-prix racing in 1977 with the first Formula 1 turbocharged racers. Their first win was in the 1979 French Grand Prix, with Jean-Pierre Jabouille.*

Niki Lauda (born 1949)

From the start of his career in a second-hand Mini-Cooper S, Niki Lauda displayed the ice-cool attitude and iron dedication that would take him to three world drivers' championships.

The tortuous 22.8km (14.2 mile) Nürburgring south of Bonn played a fateful role in his career. In 1969 he made the first-ever nine-minute lap of the circuit in a tiny, ill-handling Formula Vee racer; in 1974 he broke the seven-minute barrier while testing with Ferrari; and in 1975 – the year he won his first drivers' title – he established the all-time record of 6min 58.6sec during practice for the grand prix. The following year he led an unsuccessful campaign to boycott the Nürburgring as being too dangerous for the latest racers. Lauda's warning proved only too prophetic: in that year's grand prix at the 'Ring' his car crashed and caught fire, he breathed in searing fumes, and parts of his face were burnt almost beyond recognition. Lauda hovered between life and death for four days, before making a remarkable recovery to race at Monza only 33 days later.

After winning the title again for Ferrari in 1977, Lauda had three sterile seasons with Brabham and their sick Alfa Romeo engine, then retired.

In 1982 he returned to Formula 1 with McLaren, from whom he won a world-record retainer; he continued with McLaren in 1983 and 1984, when he won his third drivers' title in the last race of the season from team-mate Alain Prost. He retired for good in 1985.

Lauda's will to win and his obsession with the finer details of cars and circuits helped to make him one of the great test drivers of the past two decades.

Right *Lauda's 1978 protective gear included this all-enveloping helmet over a fire-resistant head-mask; a fresh-air pipe enabled him to breathe freely in event of a fire.*

INNOVATION

The 1960s and 1970s saw major advances in the design and construction of grand-prix cars. Tyres altered most visibly in width, and by the end of the 1970s the maximum wheel width permitted, 21in (550mm), led to the use of enormous rear tyres. It became customary for the front and rear tyres to be made of different compounds to improve handling; indeed, those of the two front wheels also often differed because, with races run clockwise around all the circuits, the front left tyre was subject to greater loads and wear. And then, of course, special tyres were developed for the practice sessions; and different treads were used for wet and dry conditions.

The most important design advance of the 1960s was the elimination of the chassis in favour of a monocoque (stressed-skin) structure in which the load-bearing body consisted of 'boxes' of riveted alloy sheet strengthened laterally at points along the hull. The chief strengthening elements were the floorpan, the dash panel in front of the steering wheel, the bulkhead between the driving seat and the engine, and the mountings for the suspension. The body was both stiffer and lighter than that of previous cars. In such designs even the engine acted as a stressed member and was bolted onto the rearmost box; and at least one of the suspension arms was attached to the engine casing. The first truly successful realisation of this idea was Colin Chapman's Lotus 25. The car made its debut at the 1962 Dutch Grand Prix, won five GPs that year and, in 1963, enabled Jim Clark to take the drivers' title and Lotus to clinch their first ever Constructors' Championship.

Chapman, the most innovative designer in the field of grand-prix aerodynamics and suspension systems during this period, stunned the racing world again with his 'ground-effect' Lotus 79, with which Mario Andretti and Ronnie Peterson ran away with first and second places in the drivers' championship in 1978. Ground effect involved smoothing the under-car surfaces and attaching 'skirts' to the car sides in order to give the underside the profile of a saucer. This shape had the effect of creating a vacuum between the car and the road surface, the effect increasing with the speed of the car. The vacuum 'sucked' the car down onto the road, enabling it to corner at speeds that hitherto would have been inconceivable. This radically increased performance put great strain on the structural integrity of the cars – but perhaps even greater strain on the drivers, few of whom were sorry when ground-effect designs were banned at the end of the 1982 season.

Left *Ronnie Peterson at the wheel of the revolutionary Lotus 79 'ground-effect' car. In spite of receiving fatal injuries in the Italian Grand Prix of 1978, Peterson would come second to team-mate Mario Andretti in the drivers' championship.*

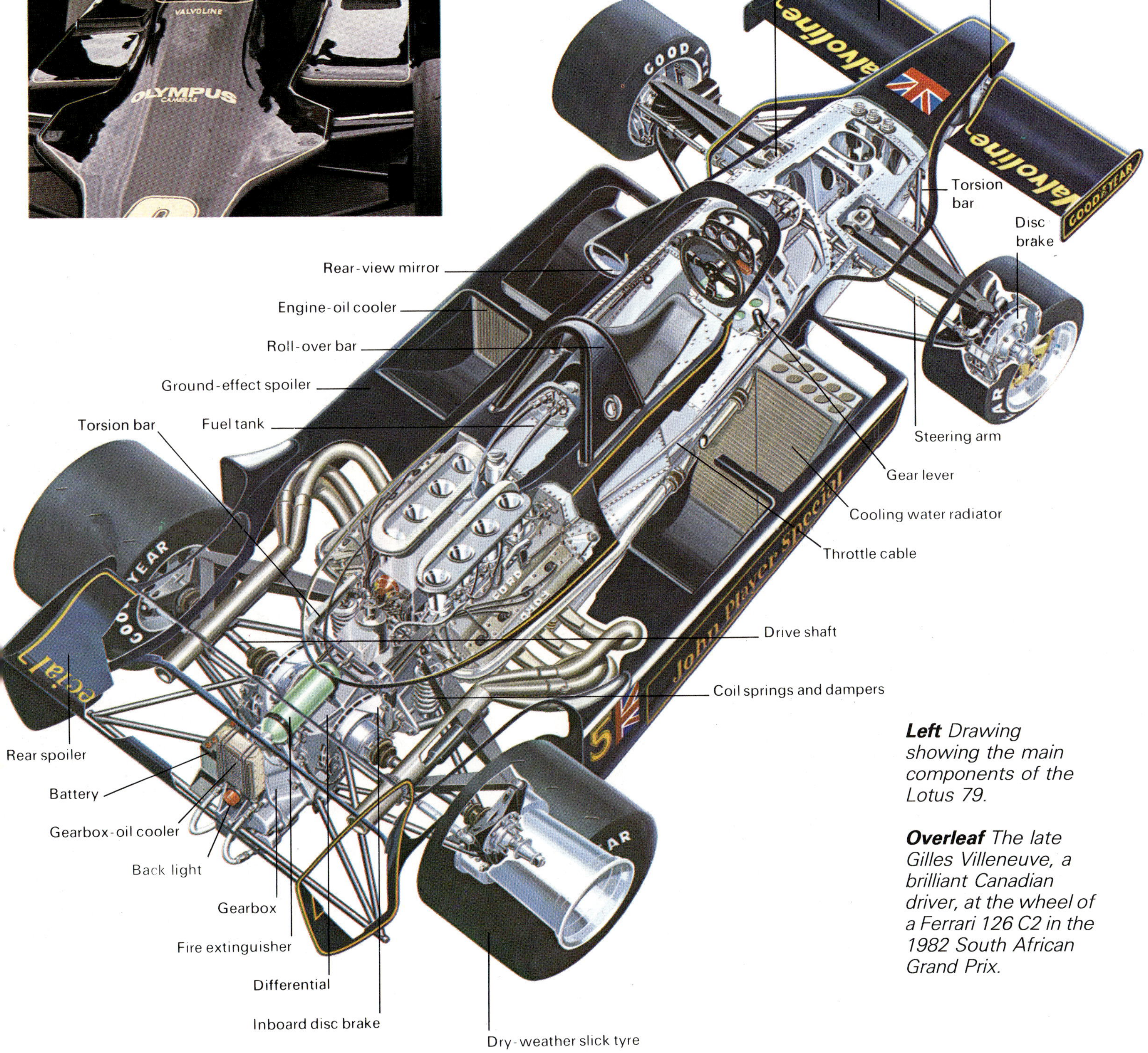

Left *Drawing showing the main components of the Lotus 79.*

Overleaf *The late Gilles Villeneuve, a brilliant Canadian driver, at the wheel of a Ferrari 126 C2 in the 1982 South African Grand Prix.*

Formula 1 Drivers' Championship 1950–86 Winners and Runners-up

1950	Giuseppe Farina (Alfa Romeo) Juan Manuel Fangio (Alfa Romeo)
1951	Juan Manuel Fangio (Alfa Romeo) Alberto Ascari (Ferrari)
1952	Alberto Ascari (Ferrari) Giuseppe Farina (Ferrari)
1953	Alberto Ascari (Ferrari) Juan Manuel Fangio (Maserati)
1954	Juan Manuel Fangio (Maserati/ Mercedes-Benz) Froilan Gonzalez (Ferrari)
1955	Juan Manuel Fangio (Mercedes-Benz) Stirling Moss (Mercedes-Benz)
1956	Juan Manuel Fangio (Ferrari) Stirling Moss (Maserati)
1957	Juan Manuel Fangio (Maserati) Stirling Moss (Vanwall)
1958	Mike Hawthorn (Ferrari) Stirling Moss (Vanwall)
1959	Jack Brabham (Cooper-Climax) Tony Brooks (Ferrari)
1960	Jack Brabham (Cooper-Climax) Bruce McLaren (Cooper-Climax)
1961	Phil Hill (Ferrari) Wolfgang von Trips (Ferrari)
1962	Graham Hill (BRM) Jim Clark (Lotus-Climax)
1963	Jim Clark (Lotus-Climax) Graham Hill (BRM)
1964	John Surtees (Ferrari) Graham Hill (BRM)
1965	Jim Clark (Lotus-Climax) Graham Hill (BRM)

1966 Jack Brabham (Repco-Brabham)
John Surtees (Ferrari/Cooper-Maserati)

1967 Denny Hulme (Repco-Brabham)
Jack Brabham (Repco-Brabham)

1968 Graham Hill (Lotus-Ford)
Jackie Stewart (Matra-Ford)

1969 Jackie Stewart (Matra-Ford)
Jacky Ickx (Ferrari)

1970 Jochen Rindt (Lotus-Ford)
Jacky Ickx (Ferrari)

1971 Jackie Stewart (Tyrrell-Ford)
Ronnie Peterson (March-Ford)

1972 Emerson Fittipaldi (Lotus-Ford)
Jackie Stewart (Tyrrell-Ford)

1973 Jackie Stewart (Tyrrell-Ford)
Emerson Fittipaldi (Lotus-Ford)

1974 Emerson Fittipaldi (McLaren-Ford)
Clay Regazzoni (Ferrari)

1975 Niki Lauda (Ferrari)
Emerson Fittipaldi (McLaren-Ford)

1976 James Hunt (McLaren-Ford)
Niki Lauda (Ferrari)

1977 Niki Lauda (Ferrari)
Jody Scheckter (Wolf-Ford)

1978 Mario Andretti (Lotus-Ford)
Ronnie Peterson (Lotus-Ford)

1979 Jody Scheckter (Ferrari)
Gilles Villeneuve (Ferrari)

1980 Alan Jones (Williams-Ford)
Nelson Piquet (Brabham-Ford)

1981 Nelson Piquet (Brabham-Ford)
Carlos Reutemann (Williams-Ford)

1982 Keke Rosberg (Williams-Ford)
Didier Pironi (Ferrari) &
John Watson (McLaren-Ford)

1983 Nelson Piquet (Brabham-BMW)
Alain Prost (Renault)

1984 Niki Lauda (McLaren-TAG)
Alain Prost (McLaren-TAG)

1985 Alain Prost (McLaren-TAG)
Michele Alboreto (Ferrari)

1986 Alain Prost (McLaren-TAG)
Nigel Mansell (Williams-Honda)

HERCULES
1
Shell

TEAMS, CARS AND DRIVERS

CREATING A WINNER

Below Williams team engineers working on a Honda F1 engine in the pit area prior to practice and qualifying sessions.

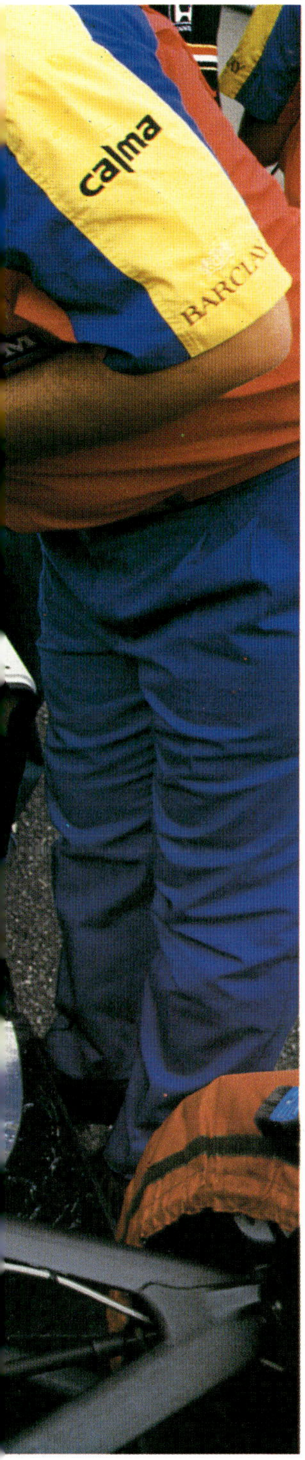

The road to developing a grand-prix winner is long and difficult, strewn with potential pitfalls set to catch out many hopeful racing-car designers. From the moment an idea begins to germinate in a designer's mind to the day the gleaming machine is pushed out into a pit lane to make its first test run, the works team will be operating flat-out in every department. Creating a car that will compete is comparatively straightforward: creating a winner is something else again.

NEW SHAPES AND MATERIALS

Until the end of the 1970s the technology of grand-prix car construction had remained little changed for more than a decade. Basically the drivers sat in 'cigars' made from aluminium alloy sheets rivetted together to enclose fuel tanks, piping and other accessories. But aerospace technology brought with it remarkable innovations such as carbon fibre, which combines great strength and remarkable lightness, and this is now the material from which every F1 racing-car chassis is made.

Working with such materials is extremely expensive, increasing the pressure on designers to make certain everything is 'right first time'. But the chassis design is an integral part of the completed car, so there may be features which the designer would like to incorporate, but is prevented from doing by other considerations.

In the days of the normally aspirated engines (until the mid-1970s) you could build an ultra-slim monocoque body hardly any wider than the Ford–Cosworth DFV V8 engine that was used by most of the grand-prix teams from the late 1960s onwards. But that was only in theory. You still needed to 'package-in' as much fuel as possible and, until the advent of a 'central' single fuel-cell immediately behind the driver, designers had fuel tanks on either side of the cockpit as well.

Once the central fuel-cell became the accepted style, other considerations prevented the evolution of pencil-slim grand-prix cars. Where were the radiators to go? In the nose section, perhaps, ahead of the drivers' feet? But that would have made the cockpit intolerably hot. What's more, radiators are heavy components, so from the point of view of the car's overall balance, the best home for them is somewhere towards the centre of the car. Hence the appearance of 'pods' on either side of the cockpit during the mid-1970s.

The next constraint on designers' talents came in the form of turbocharged engines. Although these engines were no bigger than their predecessors, the associated paraphernalia of piping, compressors and intercoolers meant that packaging a turbocharged power unit into a chassis became an unusually complex task. Fifteen years of using the Ford–Cosworth DFV had made engine installation a pretty routine affair. Now there were several brand-new turbo engines on the scene – but very little in the way of data on how they should be mated to the chassis.

Williams designer Patrick Head was faced with precisely this problem in the middle of 1983. One of the last of the top Formula 1 teams to switch from normally aspirated Ford engines, Williams signed a deal with Honda for the exclusive use of the company's turbo F1 engine. But Head had to start from scratch, with precious little technical input even from Honda, who were as new to the problem of turbo installation as Williams.

Left Patrick Head, Williams' designer, conferring with team driver Nelson Piquet after practice for the 1987 Brazilian Grand Prix at Río.

Pages 50–1 Alain Prost aboard the McLaren-TAG on his way to victory in the 1987 Brazilian GP.

CAMEL
POWERED by
HONDA
GOODYEAR
MICROMAX
CAME

When Honda delivered its first engine to Williams' factory at Didcot (Oxfordshire) it was, literally, just that – an engine. Head and his design team had to work out, through trial and error, the best positions for the turbochargers, exhaust pipes and intercoolers. It sounds a fairly routine problem: in fact it took three seasons to perfect, but it culminated in the splendid Williams FW11 which won 9 out of 16 races during 1986 in the hands of Nigel Mansell and Nelson Piquet. Then, when Honda decided to supply engines to a second team in 1987, Lotus was presented with the whole engine installation 'on a plate'. Three seasons of intensive Williams development was, in effect, handed straight over to a rival, saving Lotus an enormous amount of effort, not to mention money. It was frustrating for Patrick Head, but just one of those quirks of racing fortune which crop up from time to time.

Very seldom do designers get the opportunity to produce an entire chassis–engine package from scratch – apart, that is, from those at Ferrari whose enormous (Fiat-funded) resources mean that the famous Italian team never needs to stint on any aspect of technical detail. Nonetheless, the most spectacular example in recent times of a designer starting with a completely clean sheet of paper was the superb series of TAG turbo-engined McLarens which powered Niki Lauda and Alain Prost to the world championship in 1984 and 1985/6 respectively.

Left *Ayrton Senna in the 1987 Lotus. Powered by the Honda engine hitherto exclusive to the Williams team, the Lotus was the first car to exploit the radically new 'active-ride' suspension, giving constant ride-height under all loads.*

Marlboro
Marlboro
HERCULES
EAGLE
EAGLE

In 1982, shortly after Lauda's emergence from retirement, the McLaren team gave its chief designer John Barnard a totally free hand to produce a turbocharged F1 winner. An arrangement had been forged with Porsche to build the new engine, with backing from the Franco-Saudi high-technology group Techniques d'Avant Garde (TAG); but while the German company put its vast technical know-how into the project, it was Barnard who decided on the engine's basic configuration, mindful of the need to install it into a chassis.

The result was one of the neatest and most homogeneous F1 machines ever seen. Throughout the design process there had been very little compromise; everything in the chassis, engine and gearbox was tailor-made to work in harmony. Small wonder, then, that basically the same McLaren–TAG formula was still winning races in 1987.

Aerodynamic excellence has been one of the McLaren–TAG's strongest points. By having control of every aspect of the car's design. Barnard ensured that the air flow over the rear of the car was as unimpeded as possible, providing maximum downforce with the minimum possible drag. Others have not been so lucky over the past few years.

In 1985 Ferrari completely re-designed the turbocharger system on its wide-angle V6 engine in order to improve the aerodynamics of its new car. Until then, the Ferrari's turbos were mounted on top of the engine within the 'vee' formed by the two banks of cylinders. As a result a high engine cover was needed and this, in turn, interfered with the airflow over the rear wing. With the turbos repositioned low down on either side of the engine, below the arms of the 'vee', the engine cover could be lowered, and the car's aerodynamics improved.

Over at the Brabham team, its long-time designer Gordon Murray faced a similar problem at the end of 1984. Architect of a succession of impressive grand-prix cars, the innovative Murray designs had been compromised since 1982 by the shape of the powerful four-cylinder BMW turbo engine. The BMW unit had a tall cylinder block, so that when installed in the 1985 BT54 chassis, it too required a rather high engine cover. In turn, the cover partly masked the rear wing, reducing its effectiveness. Murray hit on a novel plan to get over this problem when design-

Opposite page *Alain Prost's McLaren-TAG MP4/3 in 'topless' form before the 1987 Belgian Grand Prix. The matt black chassis is made from carbon fibre. The quickly removable, usually one-piece, body shell is little more than an aerodynamic envelope.*

Below *Working on the McLaren-TAG MP4/3 engine in the pits at Río's Jacarepagua circuit.*

Left The BMW engine for the 1987 Brabham. It replaces the innovative but unreliable BT55 unit that made 1986 a miserable year for the Brabham team; it retains the four-cylinder configuration and, like the BT55, is laid over at an angle.

ing the new BT55. But, as so often happens when designers stray from conventional courses, what looked like a world-beater on paper turned into a disaster out on the circuits. Determined to improve the car's aerodynamics, Murray collaborated with BMW to develop a purpose-built engine laid over at an angle of 70 degrees. This enabled the car to be dramatically low, its rear wing operating in much clearer air, and pre-season opinions suggested it would be a success. Unfortunately, it wasn't. The angled engine never delivered the same performance as the upright unit it had replaced. In addition, the car had poor traction, and its drivers hated the low cockpit, which obliged them to drive with their chins tucked down on their chests. So, although the Brabham BT55's aerodynamic efficiency could be proved by reference to the speeds achieved on certain sections of certain circuits, it failed for other reasons to achieve any worthwhile race results. At the end of the year it was scrapped, to be replaced the following season by a more conventional-looking car, though still with the 'angled' BMW engine.

Interestingly, grand-prix cars often reflect the personality of their designers. The late Colin Chapman's cars were crisply to the point, brilliantly innovative, yet amazingly straightforward. He had a rare, intuitive talent that solved technical conundrums with a flash of genius. You were left wondering, if it really was that simple, why nobody had done it before. Of course, it never *was* simple: Chapman just had the gift of making it *look* like that.

Similarly, Gordon Murray's artistic inclination could be seen in the lines of his more successful Brabhams, as could Patrick Head's solid, if conservative, commonsense approach in a suc-

Below *Riccardo Patrese, Brabham-BMW's number one driver in 1986. He was joined by Derek Warwick after Elio de Angelis was killed while high-speed testing the BT55 at the Paul Ricard circuit – which as a result was considerably shortened for the French Grand Prix two months later.*

cession of Williams designs which have regularly won races over the past decade.

During his days at McLaren, John Barnard developed a reputation for demanding uncompromisingly high standards from all those who worked around him, and he himself lavished infinite care on his designs. Throughout the early 1980s the McLaren cars wanted for nothing in terms of material excellence. It cost money, of course, but in that respect the McLaren team was fortunate: while Barnard was a brilliant designer, his fellow McLaren director Ron Dennis proved wondrously adept at securing the enormous financial backing necessary to keep the show on the road.

Of course, before the first prototype is built, many hours will have been spent considering its aerodynamic specification in the most minute detail. Twenty years ago, F1 designers would put models, with tufts of cotton wool or pieces of string tacked to them, into wind tunnels to study the effects of airflow over a car – a far cry from the computer-controlled techniques employed today.

Aerodynamic testing is virtually a full-time occupation for highly qualified members of the top teams. It is not necessary, though, for John Barnard to stand watching each individual wind-tunnel test in order to reach a conclusion about an individual aspect of the design process. He can sit behind his desk in Guildford and study a computer print-out sent to him directly from the Ferrari wind tunnel at Maranello. That will tell him everything that he could have learned on a two-day trip to Italy.

ENGINE CONFIGURATIONS

As far as engine configuration during the turbo era is concerned, only TAG and Ferrari really started with an absolutely clean drawing board. Other engine makers have not been in a position of such luxury. For example, Honda's V6 configuration evolved from their successful F2 engines which dominated the European Championship in the early 1980s. BMW's four-cylinder engine has an even longer pedigree, for although it, too, was derived from an F2 unit, its ultimate origins are in the production-based touring-car units which were used as long ago as the early 1960s. Brian Hart's small factory at Harlow did a brilliant job developing its Ford-based four-cylinder turbo unit which was used by the Toleman (now Benetton) team until the end of 1985. Hart's engine was based on the light-alloy Formula 2 engine which propelled Toleman to the 1980 European Championship and which in turn evolved from technology culled from Hart's

Opposite page *The V6 engine in the 1987 Ferrari, who were hoping for greater reliability from the turbocharging unit after a disappointing 1986 season.*

Below *The Ford-Cosworth DFZ V-8 engine in the 1987 Tyrrell. With the withdrawal of the Renault V6 turbo from F1 at the end of 1986, Tyrrell decided to concentrate on normally aspirated engines.*

benetton
Arai
benetton
benetton
RIELLO
Ford
20
SISLEY

development expertise with Ford-based racing engines over the previous decade.

In 1986, when Ford decided on a completely new F1 assault, it turned again to Cosworth Engineering to produce a brand-new turbo from the ground up. The result was a compact, wide-angle V6 which, in 1987, found itself installed in the super-slim Benetton B187 designed by Rory Byrne. By common agreement among his rivals, Byrne's latest package is one of the most aerodynamically impressive to be seen this season. Achieving the lowest possible drag without losing too much downforce is the crucial equation which governs F1 at the present time: striking the most effective balance between the two is the elusive target of every designer in the game.

Alfa Romeo and Motori Moderni opted for V8 and V6 configurations respectively. Alfa never seemed to be quite certain how it wanted to conduct its F1 involvement. Initially it forged a link with Brabham from 1976–9; then it built and ran its own team of cars until the end of 1985, when it decided to miss a year's racing while development proceeded with a brand-new four-cylinder engine. A contract was signed with Ligier for its use in 1987, but the whole project screeched to a halt after the French team's number-one driver René Arnoux made some outspoken comments about the engine during a test session in Italy. Alfa Romeo promptly withdrew from racing, thereby ending a somewhat patchy period of achievement.

The Motori Moderni company is a tiny Italian firm which was originally established to build turbo engines for the equally small Minardi team. Although it is unlikely actually to win a grand prix, the combination of Minardi and Motori Moderni has proved that it is possible to compete in F1 without access to the enormous budgets consumed by the established front-line teams.

Main picture *Rory Byrne's impressive Benetton B187, in action at the 1987 Brazilian Grand Prix. The car's shape successfully creates downforce while retaining excellent aerodynamic properties.*

Inset *Ford's other Formula 1 engine, a turbocharged wide-angle V6, was first raced, as the THL2, in the 1986 Lola. The 1987 version seen here powers the Benetton.*

TESTING THE NEW CAR

All these teams and engine manufacturers eventually, of course, reach the moment of truth. After months of planning, chasing tardy component suppliers, ensuring that tyres have been delivered, double-checking that all the piping and wiring has been completed correctly, the time comes to start the engine and see if the whole thing works. To start with, the engine is run at little more than tick-over speed in the factory. As it warms up for the first time, mechanics will be examining it in minute detail, ensuring there are no unexpected leaks or obvious malfunctions. It will be warmed up to operating temperature and then switched off. It is likely that the car is then stripped down and rebuilt once more, before being taken to a circuit for its 'shakedown' run.

Finding a circuit available at the right time can be a major problem. Most British-based grand-prix teams have their new F1 cars ready for testing at the same time, in February or March. As a result, they have to go abroad to get a chance of any serious pre-season testing, since Silverstone, Brands Hatch and Donington Park are all too frequently covered with ice or snow at this time of year. Occasionally it is possible to find a decent day on which to run the car round for a few laps, but for winter testing most teams rely on the Circuit Paul Ricard, just inland from Bandol (between Marseille and Toulon), Jerez in south-west Spain, or Estoril in Portugal. Of course, there is no absolute guarantee of good weather anywhere in Europe, so there is always a 'communal' F1 test week at Río de Janeiro a month or so before the season opens with the Brazilian Grand Prix.

Assuming the car runs reliably for, say, 30 or 40 laps, the team can start thinking seriously in terms of getting down to some really high-speed testing. In most cases the drivers will be taking things easy at first – not because they have any doubts about the car's structural integrity, but because the designers and engineers have asked them to keep an eye on the instruments, to report oil pressure, temperature and so-on. Running

Right *The cramped cockpit of a modern F1 car: Alain Prost waits while engineers adjust the front suspension of his McLaren before a practice session.*

BOSS
Shell
Marlboro
Shell

Above *The front aerofoil and suspension of Nelson Piquet's Williams-Honda. Both can be finely adjusted when setting up the car for a particular circuit.*

Right *The rear wing of the 1987 Benetton-Ford. Handling of the car depends critically on the way the air passes over the car's body and onto the wing surfaces.*

gently – say five seconds or so off a really competitive time – the car will probably feel pretty good. But it is only when a top driver begins to run close to racing speed that potential problems begin to make themselves known.

The role of a racing driver in the test and development process is absolutely crucial. Although recent years have seen the use of computers to monitor engine performance, fuel-consumption and turbo-boost pressure from the pit wall, not to mention pit-to-car radio communication, ultimately a car's success depends on the driver: there is no substitute for seat-of-the-pants judgement. The most minor technical change can produce a quite violent effect on the car's performance. But only a driver can describe accurately what is happening out on the circuit.

As an example, let us go back to 1978. That gifted and versatile American Mario Andretti was then at the peak of his F1 achievement, poised to clinch the World Championship with the superb ground-effect Lotus 79. Prior to the Austrian Grand Prix, he was trying his Lotus on the very fast Österreichring circuit, carrying out comparative tests between two outwardly identical cars. One was superb, hugging the track 'like a white line', to use Mario's own words. The other was awful: it felt erratic and unstable. By the end of the day Andretti was almost tearing his hair out in frustration as he tried to get to the bottom of the problem. It seemed insoluble.

Eventually, the engineers and mechanics went through the car's detail specification with a fine-tooth comb. There was only one difference between the two machines. One had a front lower suspension arm of a slightly different shape to the other car. It was changed and, hey presto, the 'rogue' car suddenly felt as safe and secure as its stablemate. The different profile of the suspension arm, stuck out in the air stream, was affecting the airflow under the car and badly upsetting its balance. From such tiny adjustments are race winners produced!

Of course, some drivers would never have

bene

RIZIONI
Marlboro
ALBORETO
Marlboro
JEB'S
ALBORETO
Marlboro

Above Alain Prost in full 1986 racing strip. His safety harness includes both shoulder and upper leg straps.

noticed! The late lamented Ronnie Peterson, one of the greatest drivers of the post-war era, was, frankly, a hopeless test driver. But he had such a towering talent, terrific speed and split-second reflexes that, in many cases, it didn't matter. Ronnie could extract every ounce of potential from any racing car he sat in, often 'driving through' any handling imbalance to produce a tremendous race result. But such an approach was not always to the long-term benefit of the team.

THE TEST DRIVERS

In many ways, coaxing the best out of a grand-prix car is like putting together a giant jigsaw. You know all the pieces are there and you are pretty certain they will fit together. But it takes a tremendous amount of time, patience and study to end up with the right picture. This is where the top-class test driver can be worth his weight in gold. He is the man who has done the jigsaw before, knows all the short-cuts and, so to speak, puts it all together within ten minutes. And when you get a designer with a similar level of talent working with such a driver, the results can be spectacular.

In 1984, the McLaren team was fortunate enough to have all these variables working in its favour. John Barnard had designed the brilliant TAG turbo-engined MP4/2 and the team had the services of Alain Prost *and* Niki Lauda. Both men were not only excellent test drivers, but they had almost identical tastes when it came to the detailed business of 'setting-up' the chassis.

Setting-up is the detailed fine tuning of a car to an individual driver's preference. Two top line men may be able to produce the same lap times, but perhaps one likes his car to 'oversteer' slightly – that's to say, the rear wheels slide outwards slightly as he goes through a corner. But his team-mate may like a reassuring touch of 'understeer', where the front wheels are trying to slide and the driver has to apply more positive lock. Perhaps one driver likes stiff springs, the other slightly softer. And so it goes on. Prost and Lauda liked their cars set up in virtually the same style. They were also about the same size, which meant that they could share the spare car without any major adjustments, either to its handling or cockpit controls, needing to be made. Add to that the fact they were probably the two best drivers in the world and it is easy to see why McLaren won 12 out of the season's 16 races in 1984!

A good test driver will also be disciplined. He

Opposite page John Barnard (white shirt), Ferrari's chief designer from 1987, confers with Michele Alboreto during practice sessions for the San Marino Grand Prix at Imola.

will be quick enough to run a race-distance test session without losing the fine edge of his concentration. His analytical mind will be able to monitor and store up data on the car's behaviour in order to discuss it later with the engineers. The average driver will probably be able to report that a car has 'too much understeer': the talented tester will be able to report *why* it is understeering.

With two or three grand-prix distances under its belt, the new car is now ready to race. But it will not simply be tucked away in the transporter to await the first race of the year. Back at the factory it will be stripped right down to its component nuts and bolts. Everything will be examined in microscopic detail. Any potentially frail components will be strengthened or, if necessary, redesigned. Only when everything is right will the gleaming new Formula 1 challenger be rolled out into the daylight in some distant pit lane, ready for its race debut.

Out on the grid, full of fuel, the newcomer will be fussed over by mechanics like a mother hen over its chicks. Fingers will be crossed as the driver fires up the engine for the first time. Surely everything has been checked? There can't be some stupid failure now. The tension relaxes as the engine rasps into life. A quick final look-round and the mechanics return to their place behind the pit wall. Their new 'baby' is off on the parade lap.

Back in position on the grid, the field pauses momentarily. The lights on the gantry above the startline blink red. The revs rise to a crescendo. The lights blink green and the air is filled with tortured mechanical screams and clouds of dust. The field is gone, way down the track in that frantic sprint to the first corner. The designer, aerodynamicist, mechanics and everybody back at the factory have done their job. Now it's all down to the driver!

Right *The Ferrari F186 (i.e. F1, 1986), with number one driver Michele Alboreto aboard. The aerial shot shows clearly the shape of the front and rear aerofoils, the side pods and the aerodynamic body shell. The Ferrari team relies on prodigious financial backing from Fiat.*

Agip
GOODYEAR
27
LONGINES
ALBORETO
WEBER
EAGLE

FOUR SUPERSTARS

Alain Prost

Alain Prost, born on 28 February 1955 in the provincial town of St-Chamond, near Lyon, displayed the Midas touch from the very start of his career. He won the 1973 World Karting Championship and three years later dominated the European Formula Renault series, while in 1979 he took the European Formula 3 championship. The way was clearly open to grand-prix stardom. Offered a test drive for McLaren at the end of the 1979 season, he was signed on the spot by team director Teddy Mayer.

Alain scored a championship point on his F1 debut in the Argentine Grand Prix, but his first season proved generally disappointing. For 1981 he switched to Renault and immediately began to reel off victories. Yet the drivers' title eluded him, the Renault suffering a succession of mechanical failures. Finally, a major disagreement with the team saw him quit Renault a couple of days after Nelson Piquet snatched the 1983 championship from his grasp in the last race of the season.

When John Watson left McLaren, there was a vacancy in the team alongside Niki Lauda and Prost took it with hardly a moment's hesitation. It was absolutely the right choice. With its new Porsche-built TAG turbo engine now ready to race, the 1984 McLaren proved to be in a class of its own. Prost and Lauda made the championship their own private battle, but although Alain won seven races to Niki's five, the latter took the title by half a point.

In 1985 Prost made no mistakes, winning five grands-prix to clinch his long-awaited championship. His amazingly smooth driving style and mechanical empathy have marked him out as the natural successor to Lauda as the best F1 'technocrat', but his speed and consistency are such that he is now regarded as superior even to the famous Austrian. When Prost repeated the title-winning feat in the last race of the 1986 season, he became the first man to win two titles in a row since Jack Brabham in 1959 and 1960. Alain Prost already ranks as the best driver in the world. He has the temperament, style and panache to win plenty more races. A complete driver, he has no weak points – or at least none he has shown to his rivals.

***Right** At the time unquestionably the finest driver in the world, Prost won the championship in 1985 and 1986. His bid for the hat-trick in 1987 began well when (**below**) he won the championship pipe-opener in Río de Janeiro.*

DENIM
HONDA
ici
HONDA
Mobil
6
GOODYEAR
GOODYEAR
Canon

Nelson Piquet

If his father's ambitions had prevailed, Nelson Piquet might well have scaled the heights of international tennis instead of getting involved in motor racing. Born in Río de Janeiro on 17 August 1952, Nelson initially followed in his father's footsteps and became an accomplished teenage tennis player before the lure of cars, karts and motorcycles swayed his ambitions.

When Nelson returned to Brazil after a 12-month trip to California at the age of 18 he began to race karts without his family's wholehearted approval. For that reason he dropped his family name of Souto Maior and adopted the name of his mother's family for his clandestine motor racing.

After graduating quickly through the domestic Formula Super Vee class, Nelson set out for Europe at the start of 1977 to begin an international Formula 3 campaign. At the wheel of a Ralt, he limbered up by finishing third in the European Championship, preparing the way for 1978 when he took the British domestic Formula 3 scene by storm. Winning 13 races during that season, he had clinched the BP Championship before the last round, attracting a lot of interest from Formula 1 team managers in the process. He was invited to drive for the Ensign team in the German Grand Prix, where he retired, before going on to handle a private McLaren in the Austrian, Dutch and Italian races. In the last event of the year, the Canadian Grand Prix, he drove a works Brabham for the first time, laying the groundwork for a partnership which would last seven years.

After Niki Lauda retired abruptly (albeit temporarily) late in 1979, Piquet found himself elevated to team leader at the age of 27. In 1980, at the wheel of a new Ford-engined Brabham, he won his first grand prix at Long Beach (California), and went on to score triumphs in the Dutch and Italian races. Despite his novice status, he finished runner-up in the World Championship to Alan Jones.

The 1981 season saw him win his first World Championship, edging out Carlos Reutemann by a single point in a nail-biting finale at Las Vegas. Then for 1982 the Brabham team switched to BMW turbo power, which gave Piquet a mechanically troubled season with only one win. But he bounced back to snatch his second championship in 1983 after a close struggle with Alain Prost's Renault. Two relatively bleak years followed, after which he stunned the Formula 1 world by switching to the Williams–Honda squad for 1986 after Brabham boss Bernie Ecclestone failed to offer him the financial deal he wanted. Piquet came close to taking the Championship again in 1986, being eased out by Alain Prost only in the very last race of the year.

With eight years of grand-prix experience under his belt, Nelson remains as firmly committed to his chosen sport as he was when he started. Yet his intuitive skill is sometimes compromised by inconsistent performances and the occasional lapse. The way in which he ruled the roost at Río, Hockenheim and Monza in 1986 contrasted starkly with lacklustre outings at both Monaco and Estoril. Off-track, he has no interest in socialising with the motor-racing crowd and carries out only the bare minimum of promotional work for his sponsors. An assessment of Nelson's place in the F1 hall of fame will have to wait a few years yet for, despite those inconsistencies, this brilliant if moody Brazilian plans to race on for several more years.

Left *Nelson Piquet's Williams-Honda FW11 in the 1986 British Grand Prix at Brands Hatch, when he took second place to his team-mate Nigel Mansell. The Williams team ran away with the 1986 Constructors' title by a margin of no less than 46 points, brilliantly solving the problem of preparing equally competitive cars for their two star drivers, who were the keenest of rivals.*

Above *Piquet in his 1986 Williams strip – white, like the race number on his car's nose (Mansell's strip and number were red). The two drivers ran neck and neck in the title race. From 1981 to 1986 he was twice world champion, second once, and third once.*

Nigel Mansell

If sheer determination alone won world championships, Nigel Mansell would have had a stranglehold on the title for the past five years. Off-track a devoted family man, once he gets behind the wheel of a grand-prix car an all-consuming passion for success powers his whole being. What else would one expect from a man who sold his house to finance his motor racing on the way to the top – and broke his neck twice as he grappled to find a place in the grand-prix limelight?

Mansell's career began at Lucas Aerospace, where he worked on a number of projects including the RB211 jet engine, and later became a senior sales engineer at Girling before taking up motor-racing full-time. After graduating from the cut-and-thrust world of kart racing, Mansell won his first Formula Ford race at Mallory Park in 1976, and it was only another three years before he got his first F1 test, for the Lotus team,

at the Paul Ricard circuit in the south of France.

His dogged exploits in Formula Ford and later Formula 3 had been brought to the attention of Lotus boss Colin Chapman, who Mansell impressed considerably in that first F1 test. He was signed on as test and development driver for 1980 and, in the Austrian Grand Prix, was given the chance to handle a third car. Typical of his determination, he drove for much of the race in pain from petrol burns after the fuel cell split, but he refused to retire until the engine blew up.

In 1981 he was recruited full-time to the Lotus grand-prix line-up and had several promising races. But Team Lotus fortunes were at a low ebb at this time and grand-prix success continually eluded him. Chapman's faith in his talent never wavered, but the Lotus boss died suddenly from a heart attack in December 1982, and Mansell lost a valuable friend and mentor just when he needed him most.

Nigel stayed with Lotus to the end of the 1984 season; but there were times when his driving displayed a slightly desperate quality as he tried, time and again, to win his first grand prix. Success was not to come his way until 1985, after he had left Team Lotus to sign for the Williams team as second driver to Keke Rosberg.

Just as his critics were confirming their view that Mansell would never win a Formula 1 race, he triumphed in the Grand Prix of Europe at Brands Hatch. Then he won the next race in South Africa, to end the season in sixth place in the championship. He had mounted the springboard to success at last. In 1986, riding high on the crest of a wave of self-confidence, Mansell sped to five grand-prix triumphs. He lost his chance of winning the championship only when a tyre failed at maximum speed in the last race of the season. But Mansell by then had established himself as a world-class driver.

Mansell lives in the Isle of Man with his wife Rosanne and two children, Leo and Chloe. An accomplished golfer who plays off a handicap of four, one of his off-circuit ambitions is to win the British Open golf championship – but only after he has won the driver's title!

Opposite page *Nigel Mansell, unlike team-mate Piquet, had to wait the best part of five seasons for his first F1 success, late in 1985 – but he was denied the 1986 drivers' title only by a dramatic blow-out in the last race of the season.*

Below *Mansell in the Williams-Honda FW11B at the 1987 Brazilian Grand Prix.*

Below *The 1987 Lotus was (like the rival Williams) Honda-powered and by mid-season Senna was also beginning to reap the benefit of its revolutionary 'active-ride' suspension. The picture shows Senna in the Belgian Grand Prix at Spa.*

Ayrton Senna

Generally regarded as one of the most remarkable new talents to explode upon the Formula 1 scene in the last five years, Ayrton Senna's meteoric racing career can be said to have begun when he stepped into a home-made kart at the age of four! By the time he was 13, he had notched up his first official kart victory in his native Brazil. Even at this early stage of his career, Ayrton was attracting attention as an unusually committed and determined young man.

Left *Young Brazilian ace Ayrton Senna in 1987 strip.*

Born Ayrton Senna da Silva on 21 March 1960 in São Paulo, he won the South American Kart championship in 1977–80, and in 1981 moved to England to contest his first full season of Formula Ford 1600. The ease with which he swept his rivals aside to win the RAC and Townsend Thoresen titles was hugely impressive, and the margins by which he triumphed in FF2000 events the following year were so astonishing that even some F1 team managers began to take notice.

At the end of the 1982 season he won his maiden F3 race at Thruxton before returning to Brazil to line up sponsorship to enable him to take part in a complete British F3 programme the following year.

In a closely fought campaign Senna eventually edged out home boy Martin Brundle to take the title, mixing superb natural balance and car control with a self-confidence uncanny in one so young.

The Toleman team quickly snapped him up for Formula 1 in 1984 and he scored his first championship point on his second outing, in South Africa. From that point onwards his learning curve shot skywards. At Monaco, in the streaming rain, he had all but caught Prost (and had made the fastest lap) when the race was stopped prematurely; and he rounded off the year with a terrific third place behind the McLaren–TAGs in the Portuguese Grand Prix at Estoril at a time when Alain Prost and Niki Lauda were virtually toying with the opposition during their successful inter-team battle for the championship. Senna and Mansell both notched 13 points that season.

After making a somewhat awkward departure from Toleman, Senna switched to Lotus for 1985 and found a winning car beneath him for the first time. He won his second race for the team in pouring rain at Estoril, and later took the Belgian Grand Prix at Spa. Still using a Renault engine, Lotus swept him on for another couple of victories in 1986. Then Lotus's switch to the championship-winning Honda engine for 1987 promised to put Senna in machinery that was fully as competitive as the Williams and McLaren.

The index of a grand-prix driver's true talent is how he performs in the wet. In that second place at Monaco in 1984 and with the Estoril win in 1985, Senna established his F1 credentials in truly brilliant fashion. A perfectionist who sets high standards for both himself and those around him, Senna certainly has the outstanding natural ability to become one of the greatest drivers of his era. A domineering young man, whose influence over the Lotus team was sufficient to prevent them recruiting Derek Warwick as his team-mate for 1986, Senna appears aloof to some. He believes that a grand-prix weekend is a time for work and concentration, into which no frivolity is permitted to intrude.

PRACTICE

By the time a grand-prix race begins, the competing drivers know the circuit inside out. They have made mental notes of, say, a dubious strip of kerbing on the inside apex of a certain corner and where a patch of re-surfacing has made the circuit particularly slippery; worked out the best places to try out overtaking manoeuvres; and have learned how their car will perform in the early stages of the race when the fuel tank is full and the tyres not fully warmed up. They will have assimilated this information during the two days of official practice which precedes every grand-prix on the calendar.

To the outside observer, F1 practice and qualifying look like total chaos. Some cars seem forever trapped in the pit lane, apparently appearing only for the odd two- or three-lap sprint, while others seem to be lapping the circuit all the time. The reality of the situation is that every team is operating to a carefully worked-out plan of action, hopefully ending up with its cars on the front row of the starting grid for Sunday's race.

In recent years, practice and qualifying have evolved into a standard format. On the Friday and Saturday before the race (Thursday and Saturday at Monaco) there is an untimed session, which does not count for grid positions, each

__Below__ The Williams pit during practice sessions before the 1986 Mexican Grand Prix. If two spare cars are available, each is allocated to a particular driver and is set up in exactly the same way as his race car.

Left *A Goodyear engineer checks the temperature of Mansell's front tyres. Each grand-prix circuit has a different effect on tyres in terms of wear and running temperature, and different tyre compounds are tried in the search for optimum performance.*

morning from 10.00 to 11.30. Then there is an hour of official qualifying from 13.00 to 14.00. Finally, on race morning, there is a half-hour warm-up session just to make final checks and adjustments prior to the start of the grand prix.

Since the start of the 1987 season Goodyear has had a tyre-supply monopoly in Formula 1, and each team is allotted eight sets of tyres per car per race. Only two of these sets can be used by each car during the timed qualifying sessions. This regulation was originally introduced to prevent teams using an unlimited number of super-sticky qualifying tyres in the days when Goodyear, Michelin and Pirelli were all battling for victory in the F1 arena. With Goodyear assuming the task of supplying all the teams, qualifying tyres were no longer produced, but the limit of two sets per car per session was retained. And to make sure nobody cheats, those two nominated sets per car are painted with the stencilled car's race number on their sidewalls. Each time the car leaves the pit lane it must pass four marshals who check that it is using tyres marked with the correct number.

A team may well have availed itself of some pre-race testing at a given circuit prior to race weekend but, in general, that will have provided only a broad base of information: changes of temperature, or even such an apparently minor matter as a change in the wind, can affect a car's performance 'on the day'. And of course the surface of each circuit is different from all the others in a variety of ways.

The first unofficial session sees most teams 'limbering up' in preparation for the serious business of the afternoon. There may be a new gearbox which needs running in, or a minor change of suspension geometry which has been fitted to the spare car so that a driver can assess whether it is an improvement over the set-up on his race car. This 'back to back' testing often provides an invaluable short-cut to improved

Left *Changing the ratios of the gears on a Ferrari F187 during the first unofficial practice session for the 1987 Monaco Grand Prix. Each F1 circuit requires a different combination of gears; the slow, many-cornered Monaco circuit calls for lower gearing than the faster tracks such as the Österreichring and Silverstone.*

Right *Michele Alboreto (Ferrari F186) confers with his pit team during practice for the 1986 San Marino Grand Prix. Fifth fastest qualifier, Alboreto was denied fourth place in the race by turbocharger failure, Ferrari's greatest bugbear during the 1986 championship.*

performance and is carried out by virtually every team that can afford to have a spare car on hand for the weekend.

There is also the question of sizing up the opposition. It may be that one of the teams has made some sort of technical break-through since the last race. The untimed Friday morning session can be useful to the other teams in assessing the effects of that improvement. Of course, the team in question may play a cautious game, unwilling to show their hand before the second timed qualifying session on Saturday afternoon. One of the fascinations of the practice sessions for experienced observers of the sport lies in detecting the gamesmanship indulged in by the various teams.

By the end of the first 90-minute session, the drivers will be getting into the swing of things and running quite quickly. But they may well have decided that they need a change of gear ratios before the first qualifying session; or perhaps an engine has lost a few revs at high speed, suggesting that it is in need of replacement. So the lunch-box between the two sessions is anything but restful for the mechanics. While they slave away changing gear ratios, springs and ride heights, the driver will probably be in deep discussion with the engineers and, possibly, the designer. Should they leave that engine in for first qualifying and change it tonight? Is the spare car ready in case they have a failure? Perhaps they could move the steering wheel a little closer? Is there any way in which they could move the brake-balance control down a bit in the cockpit? – the driver might be grazing it with his knuckle when he locks over into a hairpin. So the complaints, debates and discussions go on.

QUALIFYING LAPS

If everything is running well, the top teams will be seen moving at least one of their cars down the pit lane about 10 minutes before the start of first qualifying. The driver, helmet and gloves already on, will sit motionless in the cockpit waiting for the track to open. These teams have decided to 'go early'. That is to say, their drivers will attempt

Below *An engineer makes an adjustment to the suspension of a 1986 Arrows-BMW A8. As with the selection of gearbox ratios, fine tuning of the suspension for a particular circuit depends greatly on the reports of the driver during practice sessions.*

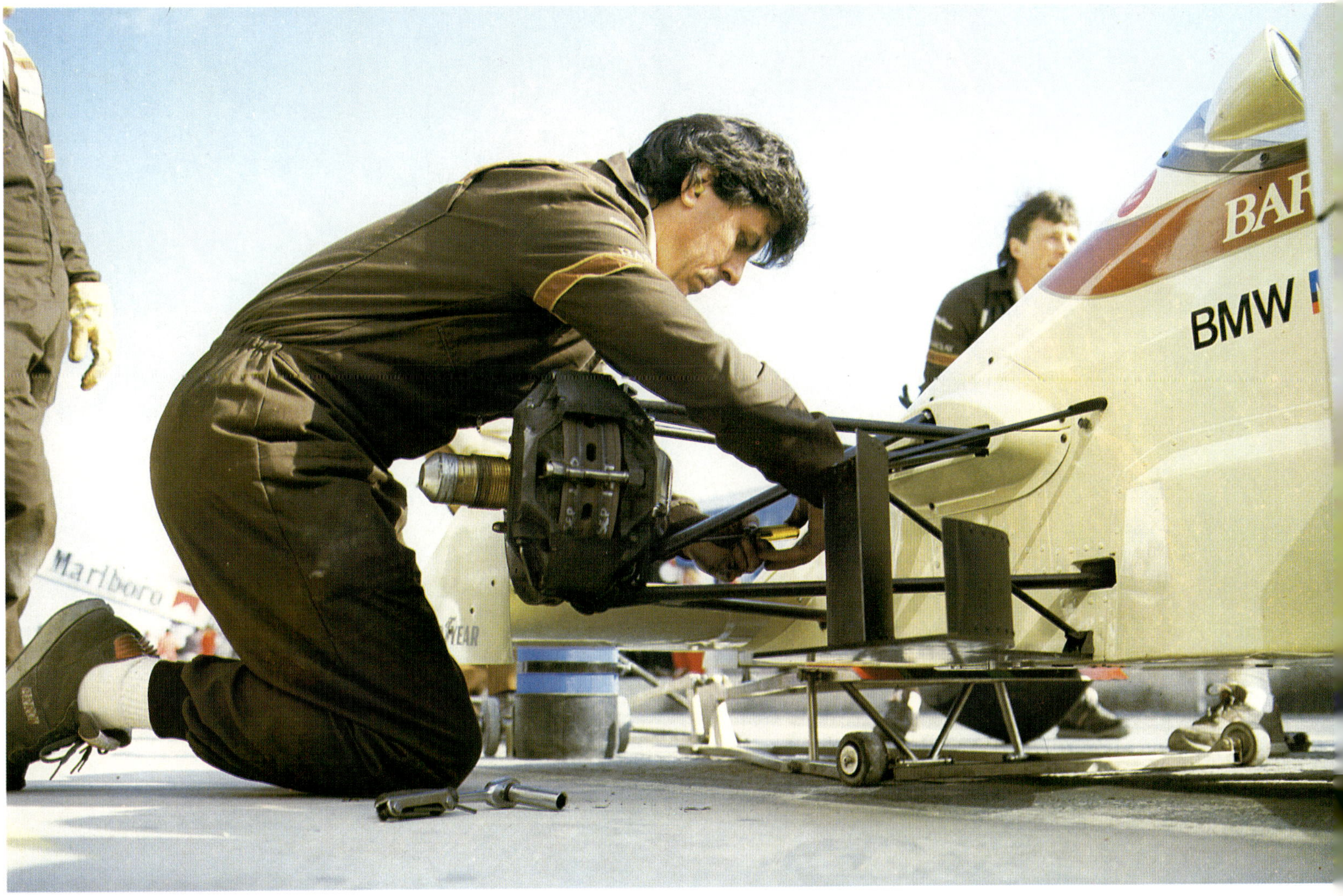

Above Ayrton Senna (Lotus-Honda) in the 1987 Brazilian Grand Prix, the first F1 race of the season. With a new engine (albeit one race-developed by Williams) and radically new suspension, Lotus's practice sessions before the race were scrutinized even more carefully than usual by their rivals.

to capitalise on a relatively traffic-free circuit to get a fast qualifying lap under their belt before too many other cars are out there to get in the way. Once this has been achieved, they often retire to the pits and watch, hawk-like, to see who goes quicker before they make their second run. Each team is connected up to the official electronic timing system which records the lap times during qualifying – and during the race itself – so each team knows what the others are doing.

Farther back down the pit lane you may see a driver such as Ayrton Senna take his helmet off after a quick, early run and loll against the pit wall as if he hasn't a care in the world. But don't be fooled into thinking that he is not watching. The chances are that he will be monitoring every rival's move with eagle-eyed accuracy and, when he walks casually back across the pit lane to his car, you just *know* that something spectacular is about to happen. Senna is one of those inspired performers who can extract the ultimate from a grand-prix car in any given situation. But watching him prepare for a really quick qualifying lap is like watching as an orchestra works itself up to a controlled frenzy for the spectacular finale of a symphony.

To start with, the pace seems gentle, almost casual. But if you watch closely, you will see that the team is a disciplined, skilfully interlocking group of like-minded individuals. Senna will have made a mental note of where all his rivals are on the circuit: 'Prost has done his two runs, so no need to worry about him; Mansell's race car stopped out on the circuit, so he's using the spare – which seems to be in the pits with gearbox trouble; the Ferraris . . . yes, I can deal with them. That leaves the quick Brabham and two Benettons. Right, I'll go now. . . .'

One mechanic will have pumped fuel out of the spare Lotus, which has now been set up in

Right *A nap-hand of Honda engines in the Lotus pit. Spare engines are essential because even two units meticulously prepared by the same engineers may reveal quite different characteristics during practice sessions.*

LONGINES
watches
OS N. DRIVER TIME LAP NL
1 17 C. DANNER 1'34.473 11 23
2 4 P. STREIFF 1'34.887 3 9
momo
TEAM LOTUS
LAP
OFF
bar

'qualifying' specification: it needs only the bare minimum of fuel for a three-lap run; it is fitted with weight-saving carbon-fibre brake discs; the turbo boost pressure will be turned up as high as it can be without 'tripping' the mandatory boost-control valve. Now Senna climbs aboard. His belts are tightened. And he's away. . . .

Remember, he has only a few laps before the tyres begin to lose the fine edge of their grip, so he needs to grab as traffic-free a lap as possible while he still has maximum adhesion. That can sometimes be difficult. Senna and his rivals must balance risk against realism: he must judge expertly whether he can overtake a certain car going into a certain tricky corner, while relying on his rival's judgement not to move over on him.

Suddenly, Senna is on his fastest lap. The air is almost alive with excitement as he slams round the circuit, trips the timing beam and eases off the throttle. Just as suddenly it is all over. Maybe he has set the fastest time; perhaps only second fastest. Word comes down the pit lane: 'Prost is fastest'. The World Champion's rivals shake their heads. English driver Martin Brundle shrugs: 'You know, in my three years of Formula 1, I have *never* seen Prost on what looked like a qualifying lap. He's just so smooth nobody's ever aware he is going quickly. Or do they just give him pole position as a matter of course?' Everybody laughs – but in 1986 it was Senna who was the undoubted pole 'king'.

At 14.00 on Friday it is all over until tomorrow. Cars are pushed back into their pit garages and drivers disappear with their team managers into motorhomes to 'de-brief'. This means they go through the day's work in lap-by-lap detail, probing each other's thoughts, analysing the times, speculating where time might be lost or gained. Meanwhile, the mechanics are maybe taking a few minutes off for a well-earned sandwich and a drink. But their work could well go on for several hours more.

After an hour or two, the engineers emerge from the de-brief and confer with the chief mechanics. A job list is produced to cover all the changes that need to be made to the team's cars before Saturday practice begins. These can range from routine, if lengthy, tasks such as an engine or gearbox change, to more complex work. Perhaps one engine has a mysterious misfire which has proved impossible to cure. There may be a

Left *Senna checks the lap times of his rivals before putting in a qualifying lap on the second practice day. The VDU shows a read-out from the official electronic timing system which records lap times during both qualifying and the race proper.*

Above *Alain Prost and Keke Rosberg at a debriefing session during qualifying for the 1986 Monaco Grand Prix. White-shirted McLaren team manager Ron Dennis is behind Prost, who later drove brilliantly to take first place in the race, Rosberg following him home to take second place – his best result of the season.*

problem in its electrical circuits, so it may have to be totally stripped.

Another car may have a tricky fuel-system problem – perhaps the fuel pump just will not pick up the last few gallons when the fuel load goes down. That really is a major drama, because with only 195 litres (about 43 gallons) of fuel permitted by the regulations, every eggcupful counts in the race. The problem must be rectified in time for Saturday practice, so the whole fuel cell may have to be changed. That is a long job.

In addition, there is routine maintenance to be carried out. Suspension components have to be checked, all the cockpit instruments are looked over. The electrical system will be examined by mechanics with the patience and care of a surgeon carrying out a delicate operation.

PRACTICE: DAY TWO

Come Saturday morning and it's as though Friday never happened. With that sense of unquenchable optimism which you need to survive in as demanding a world as grand-prix racing, everybody is up early and raring to go. The previous day's trials and tribulations are being swept to the back of everybody's minds. Saturday's untimed morning session almost certainly sees many cars running with full fuel loads. This enables the teams to get some idea of what sort of fuel-consumption figures they can expect for the following day's race. It also helps decide what gear ratios to use and, also, how best to set up the car's ride height.

A racing-car's gearbox bears little resemblance to that in a family saloon. Most top teams use six-speed gearboxes which are specially designed and built for the individual car in which they are used. More importantly, the gear ratios can be changed in an hour or so in order to get the very best performance out of an engine on any given circuit. The demands of a gruelling street circuit such as Monaco or Detroit, for instance, are quite different from those of the ultra-fast tracks such as the Österreichring or Silverstone.

On tight circuits, low gears are fitted to produce

Right *McLaren engineers working on the MP4/3, the 1987 version of the TAG engine. By mid-season, the Williams-Honda was clearly the fastest car on the F1 circuits, only the McLaren's chassis and Prost's superlative skills keeping his team in contention.*

Marlboro
MP4/3
BOSS

CAMEL
HONDA

the best acceleration out of tight corners. The hill up to Casino Square at Monaco is steep (about 1 in 8) and the cars need as much 'punch' as possible to sprint up to the top in double-quick time. Maximum speed is of less importance than on a really fast circuit where high gears are fitted to the cars, enabling them to accelerate smoothly in fifth and sixth gears towards their maximum potential speed without over-revving the engine. A car with a top gear suitable for the 150mph dash through the curving tunnel at Monaco would be over-revving madly if asked to do 190mph at Silverstone. That would not only risk damaging the engine but, just as important, ruin its fuel-consumption figures, so that it could well run out of fuel before the end of the race. It might be thought that, with six gears at his disposal, a designer could produce a gearbox suitable for all circuits. But sports cars of every kind, and racing-cars especially, need what is called a close-ratio box, in which the ratio of one gear does not differ greatly from those of the gears immediately below and above it. Such a box, given slick gear-changing, provides better acceleration than one whose gear ratios are widely spaced.

Even a change in the wind can affect the car's performance and require subtle adjustment of the gears. In Saturday's untimed session there may be a headwind on the main straight. On the face of it, that means a lower sixth gear in order that the car can 'pull' harder against the gale. But, if such a change is made during the lunch break, that car could well find itself over-revving if the head wind changes to a tail wind before qualifying starts!

All these considerations have to be taken into account and a compromise reached. Similarly, deciding on the car's optimum ride height can be fraught with difficulty. 'Ride height' is the crucial gap between the underside of the car and the surface of the track; in the interests of good

Left *Peter Wright and Lotus colleagues running a computer test on Senna's suspension. On today's F1 cars, ride height (the gap between the car's underside and the road) is crucial to the car's handling and aerodynamics. With a full tank of fuel, the ride height may be less than one inch. The new 'active-ride' suspension maintains constant ride height under all loads.*

roadholding, handling, and aerodynamic efficiency, the gap must be as small and as unvarying as possible.

Of course, if a car is set up with its ride height at **1g** inches with a full fuel load aboard, this may well increase to two inches once the fuel load is consumed and the car becomes lighter. So another compromise is required. With a full load of fuel aboard, the car may well be set up with a ride height of only half an inch. That guarantees that, as the fuel load lightens, the car will rise slightly to somewhere near its optimum ride height. During practice and qualifying and the early stages of a race, you can always tell the cars that are running with a full fuel load by the trail of sparks as they 'bottom out', their undersides hitting the track whenever they go over a bump. Recent developments have centred on 'active-ride' computer-controlled suspension to maintain a constant ride height. In 1987 Lotus were early leaders in this department.

The final Saturday qualifying session turns into a far more frenzied affair than that on the previous afternoon. For those drivers who had technical trouble on Friday, this is their last chance to improve their qualifying time. Again, only two marked sets of tyres per car are permitted, and this rule is strenuously enforced. It is permissible for a driver to do two runs and then go out again on a mixed set of tyres, the best used pair from each of his previous two sets, but no more than eight tyres per car must be used. If a driver should be unfortunate enough to suffer a puncture, that is his misfortune. No replacement tyres are allowed.

POLE POSITION

The objective of all this effort is to qualify for 'pole' position – that is, the number one starting position on the grid. The cars line up for the grand prix start in pairs, the faster of each pair 'staggered' slightly ahead of the other. Pole position is thus slightly forward of the second place qualifier on the opposite side of the track.

The benefits are innumerable. The most obvious empty track ahead of him. If he makes a good

Right *Last-minute checks to Nelson Piquet's Williams-Honda FW11 before he sets out on his final qualifying lap. The front and rear aerofoils, side pods and cramped cockpit are typical of all present-day F1 cars. Note also the slick (treadless) tyres.*

Canon
Canon
FIBERITE
ICI
DENIM

PIRELLI
elf
GITANES

advantage is that the pole-position man has an start and can sustain the pace, he has a good chance of leading throughout, especially on city-street circuits where it is very difficult to overtake. Second, the pole-position man usually starts on the side of the track offering the best possible line through the first corner. This will not necessarily be the best line when he is racing hard and approaching the corner at speed; but from a standing start he will arrive at the corner more slowly, and he may well be able to snatch an early advantage.

Prestige, of course, has its part to play. There is a psychological advantage in starting from pole position which, in some cases, has a driver's rivals beaten almost before the start. But it is not a position without its responsibilities.

Before the start, there is a formation (or parade) lap away from the grid. The cars return, line-up, and are then unleashed by the green starting light. The pole-position man is the one from whom everybody else takes their lead. He must lead them round the parade lap not too quickly, and not too slowly. Running too quickly may heap problems on himself. If he arrives back on pole position too soon, he may have to sit waiting with the engine running for longer than is ideal. That might result in the first signs of engine overheating; it also uses up precious fuel.

On the other hand, if he goes too slowly, the pack behind will crowd in on him, become edgy and over-anxious and, as a result, perhaps get away at the green light to a ragged start which can cause all sorts of problems from banging wheels to a multiple pile-up.

The routine after second qualifying is much the same as the previous afternoon. The drivers emerge from the debriefs either elated or de-

Left *Fuelling up Philippe Alliot's Ligier-Renault JS27 before the start of the 1986 Hungarian Grand Prix. Each car is permitted 195 litres and the fuelling is carefully monitored by race officials. Alliot, replacing Jacques Laffite, injured in the British Grand Prix, took a creditable ninth place at Budapest.*

pressed, depending on their qualifying positions, and comments to the mechanics range from 'I want this, that and something else changed' to 'Please don't touch it. It's absolutely perfect!'

The fastest 26 cars start the race, except at Monaco where the field is usually restricted to 20. If more have taken part in practice, that's bad luck. The 27th competitor, however, always takes part in the race-morning warm-up, just in case something happens to one of the other competitors.

Saturday night is the toughest for the mechanics. Many teams change the engine on all their cars, using the new ones for the following day's race and then during qualifying for the next grand prix on the calendar. All the knowledge and experience gained during the two previous days is considered, distilled in the engineers' minds and then minutely analysed yet again. After this deliberation is complete, the final detailed set-up for the car will be specified.

On race morning, the half-hour warm-up session is usually the most reliable indicator of form in the race to follow. All the cars will be running in race trim, with no qualifying 'tweaks'. Suddenly it may become apparent that Prost, who has perhaps only qualified fourth on the grid, is easily the quickest. He could be the man to watch when it comes to the serious business of the weekend.

These race-morning sessions are not without their dramas. An engine failure now produces what, to the outsider, looks like acute panic. Mechanics fall on the car and begin a lightning engine change to prepare the car for the race. It may look like a circus but, in fact, most teams work to a prescribed routine in such circumstances. They work fast, but with great accuracy.

Finally the moment arrives. The cars are fuelled up and wheeled out to the starting grid. That two days of frantic activity is over. All that remains is the 200 mile sprint to the chequered flag.

By the end of the afternoon, some will be elated, others dejected. Either way, they will be back at another circuit two weeks later, starting all over again with the same glimmer of optimism in their eye. This time, surely, it will be different!

Right *The 26 qualifying cars line up on the starting grid at Imola for the 1987 San Marino Grand Prix. Senna is in pole position – he had also taken pole in eight of the 16 races in 1986, including San Marino. Nigel Mansell and Alain Prost are next on the grid.*

ES LO
Marlboro
Marlboro
CAMEL
West
MOËT

FOUR TO WATCH

Gerhard Berger

At the end of the 1985 season, after a year with the Arrows team, it was by no means certain that Gerhard Berger would be staying in grand-prix racing the following year. Unquestionably, he had the talent and ability. But in such a high-powered world, sponsorship considerations do not always take such factors into account.

Happily, the genial 27 year old from Worgl, near Innsbruck, found a vacant niche in the Benetton-BMW squad. Less than 12 months later he was standing on the victory rostrum at Mexico City, having just scored the team's maiden grand-prix success. And six weeks after that he had signed to drive for the most famous team in the business – Ferrari.

By any standards, Berger's progress through the motor-racing ranks has been meteoric. He first sprang to prominence in the European Alfasud championship, finishing seventh in the contest at his first attempt. Formula 3 followed in 1983 with Gerhard quickly demonstrating considerable promise and prowess in this hotly contested category. Although he did not win one of the European Championship rounds, he did manage a couple of second places to finish joint seventh in the points table, equal with Martin Brundle.

Berger then tackled the European Touring Car Championship, where his spectacular form at the wheel of the BMW 635 coupés attracted the attention of the ATS Formula 1 team. He drove for them in the 1984 Austrian Grand Prix and, although he failed to finish at Zeltweg, a few weeks later he stormed home an impressive sixth in the Italian Grand Prix at Monza. (The fact that he was not originally registered as one of the season's regular F1 contestants precluded his being awarded the single point which goes to the driver taking sixth place.)

It seemed that new vistas of opportunity were opening up for Gerhard, but his racing career very nearly ended when he was involved in a serious road accident near his home in Austria shortly after the end of the season. Fortunate to escape with fractured vertebrae in his neck, he spent most of the winter recuperating. But he was well enough to join Thierry Boutsen in the Arrows-BMW squad at the start of the 1985 Championship season and rounded off that year with a fifth place in South Africa and sixth in Australia.

In 1986 he really began to mature, handling the Benetton-BMW with such flair and expertise that it was easy to forget he had less than two seasons' F1 experience. He led his home grand prix commandingly at the Österreichring until he was forced into the pits with battery problems; but he judged things superbly in the searing heat of Mexico to win that country's grand prix, thanks to a non-stop run on Pirelli rubber – when all his Goodyear-shod rivals were having to stop two or even three times.

He then made the decision to join Ferrari. There had been an offer to become Alain Prost's team mate at McLaren (Keke Rosberg having retired) – but no, he wanted to drive for Ferrari. Like his driving the choice was both cool and emotional – he had a passionate desire to be associated with the Prancing Horse, as every driver does at one time or another. Gerhard has probably joined at a good time. This relaxed, extrovert, genial young man has an informal off-track manner which belies his true skill in the cockpit. He could well become one of the great ones.

Below, left *Gerhard Berger's total of 17 championship points (one first, one third, one fifth and two sixths) in 1986 for the Benetton team took him to seventh place in the drivers' championship and earned him an offer few up-and-coming F1 drivers could refuse – an invitation to join the Ferrari team for 1987. He's seen here in his new colours.*

Below *Berger in the Ferrari F187 at the 1987 Brazilian Grand Prix. Berger joined Michele Alboreto in the Italian* équipe*, Stefan Johansson having left to become Prost's partner at McLaren-TAG in succession to Keke Rosberg.*

West
West
FANATIC
West
Castrol
BOSCH
BBS
GOODYEAR
FANATIC

Martin Brundle

An equable chap from King's Lynn (Norfolk), Martin Brundle has always given the impression of having his feet firmly planted on the ground. Whether battling with Ayrton Senna in the cut and thrust of Formula 3, handling Jaguar's XJS coupés in the European Touring Car Championship, or learning the ropes about F1 during three seasons with Ken Tyrrell's team, Brundle has demonstrated a mix of cunning and good judgement which could well see him rise to the top of his chosen sport.

Brundle was born into a world of fast cars and motorsport. His family owns a Toyota dealership in King's Lynn and his father was a keen amateur rally driver. After cutting his teeth on saloon cars, Brundle junior began making a name for himself in British F3 in 1982, and finished runner-up to Ayrton Senna in that series the following year, the two men carving up the wins between them in an impressive display of their future F1 promise.

At the end of 1983 Brundle was offered a seat in the Tyrrell F1 team, a glittering reward for his F3 efforts. He was not asked to contribute a single penny to Ken's budget, but signed for three years. Initially he handled a non-turbo Ford-Cosworth-engined car, but after a fine second place behind Nelson Piquet in Detroit, he crashed during practice for the Dallas Grand Prix, sustaining leg and ankle injuries which put him out for the rest of the season. For 1985 Tyrrell signed a contract to use Renault engines in his cars, so Brundle sampled turbo power for the first time the following summer.

Steadily, he consolidated a reputation as a promising performer, staying with Tyrrell through to the end of 1986. He had started the season in excellent style with fifth place in the Brazilian Grand Prix, and ended it with a flourish, achieving his best finish (4th) with the Renault-engined car in the last race of the year in the Australian Grand Prix at Adelaide.

After three years, when his contract expired, Brundle decided to join the German Zakspeed team. He was impressed by the technical ingenuity demonstrated by this small organisation and his decision to switch camps was rewarded in only the second race of the 1987 season when he finished a fine fourth in the San Marino Grand Prix at Imola.

Away from the circuits, Martin enjoys clay-pigeon shooting and private flying, but his top priority is keeping himself in tip-top physical trim for his chosen profession. Married to Liz, he still lives close to his old home, preferring familiar surroundings to tax exile abroad. That in itself mirrors his straightforward and sensible nature – personal qualities well calculated to ensure survival in the high-pressure grand-prix world.

Above *Martin Brundle aboard the Zakspeed in the 1987 Belgian Grand Prix at Spa. Rapidly acclimatising himself to his new car and to the small but ambitious German team, Brundle achieved a fine fourth place in the San Marino Grand Prix.*

Inset *Brundle, seen here in his 1987 driving strip, joined Zakspeed after three years with Tyrrell. Prior to that he had enjoyed two superb seasons in F3 racing.*

Below *Thierry Boutsen's new mount for 1987 – the Rory Byrne-designed Benetton B187, powered by the new V6 Ford-Cosworth turbocharged engine. One of the most impressive-looking cars on the circuit in 1987, the B187 had still to establish itself as truly competitive against the might of the Williams, Lotus, and McLaren teams.*

Right *Boutsen, having spent three years with the Arrows team variously partnering Berger, Marc Surer and Christian Danner, leapt at Peter Collins' invitation to drive for Benetton after Berger's departure to Ferrari.*

Thierry Boutsen

There is something about Thierry Boutsen that exudes star quality in abundance. He is a good-natured 30-year-old with impeccable manners and a gentle demeanour. But out on the track he is absolutely uncompromising in battle, while retaining a driving style which is as immaculate as his always-crisp, freshly laundered overalls.

Attracted to the sport by the exploits of fellow Belgian Jacky Ickx, Boutsen's first real taste of the business came when he attended the racing drivers' school at Zolder at the age of 18. By 1977 he had managed to buy his own car, an elderly Formula Ford Hawke, but it was not until 1978 that he really began to make his mark. At the wheel of a Crossle, he won 15 out of the 18 races he contested, clinching the Benelux Championship before moving into Formula 3 the following year.

In 1980 he finished second behind Michele Alboreto in the European F3 Championship at the wheel of a Martini. From there his career progressed into Formula 2 in 1981, when he won a couple of races in a March-BMW before joining the Spirit-Honda team the following year.

When Honda nominated the Spirit team to try out its prototype turbocharged grand-prix engine in 1983, Boutsen hoped he would be the one nominated to race it. He was to be disappointed, that privilege falling to his team-mate Stefan Johansson. Undaunted, he raised sufficient sponsorship to clinch a contract with the Arrows team, for which he first raced in the 1983 Belgian Grand Prix at Spa.

The limitations of his machinery kept Boutsen's talent largely concealed over the next three seasons, although it was there for the experts to see if they really looked. The superb way he held down fourth place at Spa in 1985 until his machine wilted with mechanical failure a couple of laps from the finish gave undeniable evidence of his true ability and potential. Boutsen also excelled at the wheel of Porsche sportscars and his victory over the works Jaguars in the Spa endurance race at the end of 1986 helped sustain his reputation on the F1 driver market.

Benetton team manager Peter Collins had never doubted Boutsen's talent so, when he became available at the end of his Arrows contract, he was quickly snapped up to fill the slot left vacant by Berger's switch to Ferrari at the start of 1987.

Boutsen is a cool customer. His equable temperament ensures that he never allows himself to get ruffled even in the heat of a really close Formula 1 battle. Moreover, he has a delicate and sympathetic touch with the machinery. Modest he may be, but Thierry Boutsen could go all the way to the top if the Benetton becomes genuinely competitive.

Jonathan Palmer

Known affectionately amongst his peers as 'the Doc', Jonathan Palmer's level-headed attitude towards motor-racing is reflected by the fact that he completed his medical training and qualified as a doctor before tackling a full-time career in professional motor racing. Born in 1957, he qualified in 1979 and held two hospital posts before relinquishing his medical career and becoming involved with fast cars.

He had originally been introduced to the sport through his father, Dr Jack Palmer, who had been Chief Medical Officer for the British Automobile Racing Club. Jonathan began racing with an Austin-Healey sports car in 1975 before switching to Formula Ford. In 1981 he won one of the coveted Grovewood Awards, presented to young British drivers who show outstanding promise, and then set himself firmly on the path to international recognition by clinching the 1982 British Formula 3 Championship in fine style. In 1982 he moved up into F2, won the European Championship the following year, and made his grand-prix debut in the third Williams in the 1983 Brands Hatch Grand Prix of Europe.

In 1984 he signed for the RAM team for his first full F1 season, switching to Zakspeed for 1985 and 1986. Both were relatively small and moderately-financed teams, with little more racing experience in the top league than Jonathan himself. None the less, 'the Doc' proved himself a cool, methodical racer whose orderly mind and clear-sighted approach helped him gain a worthwhile reputation as a test and development driver.

Palmer's first full F1 season was interspersed with a successful programme of sportscar racing for the privately fielded, British-based Richard Lloyd Porsche team in the World Sportscar Championship. At the end of 1986 he took a gamble. Anxious to promote his career at the highest possible level, he held out on the off-chance that he might be offered the second McLaren drive alongside Alain Prost. Sadly, it was a vain hope: the drive went to Stefan Johansson. Meanwhile, fellow Englishman Martin Brundle had been signed up as his replacement at Zakspeed, briefly leaving Palmer out in the wilderness until his career was rescued by the chance to drive for Ken Tyrrell.

Although Tyrrell's cars were contesting only the non-turbo 'second division' class in F1 during 1987, Palmer immediately proved as fast and determined as any of his rivals in this category. More impressively, he had absolutely no qualms about taking a step backwards in order to consolidate his career. He hopes in the long run to be able to take two or three steps forward as a result.

Mature, sensible and well-balanced, Palmer has a calm exterior which belies the steely determination which lurks beneath the surface. Given a competitive car, he could find himself on the winner's rostrum in a couple of seasons.

Above *Jonathan Palmer in 1987 Tyrrell strip. He and Brundle swapped équipes at the end of 1986 after Palmer had proved himself a gifted test and development driver in his two seasons with the Zakspeed team.*

Right *Palmer driving the Tyrrell-Ford DG016 in the 1987 Brazilian Grand Prix. Later, at Monaco, he drove a fine race to earn his first-ever championship points.*

Data General
Data General
COURTAULDS
COURTAULDS
Data General
Tyrrell
Data General
3

IN THE PITS

Watching the action on a television screen, you might well be forgiven for concluding that the average Formula 1 pit lane is nothing more than a disorganised jumble of men and machines. In fact, nothing could be further from the truth. Crowded it may well be on race day, but beneath that appearance of terminal frenzy everything is planned out with meticulous care and carried out with military precision.

The pit lane is the operational heart of the grand prix, functioning in much the same way as, for example, a military airfield controls its fighter planes. It is in the pit lane garages that the cars are prepared before a day's practice or racing, and it is to those garages that they return at the end of the action. All the time, they are tended by and worried over by a squad of highly trained and single-minded mechanics.

In the past few years the sport's governing body, FISA, has laid down stringent pit specifications which must be adhered to by circuits wishing to stage world championship-qualifying grands prix. But if we go back 20 years or so, the life of a Formula 1 mechanic was gruelling, to say the least. Criss-crossing Europe before the current motorway network was anything like complete, the mechanics travelled cramped into often old, slow and unreliable transporters. When it came to preparing the cars at the circuits, the work was often carried out in the open, irrespective of whether it was hot or cold, wet or dry. Engine, gearbox and suspension components could be seen scattered over the paddock surface around the car. If they were lucky, the mechanics might get a sandwich and a cup of coffee before their toil ended at around midnight.

How different things are today. Top grand-prix teams move their cars and equipment round Europe in luxurious, purpose-built transporters which are designed and equipped with all the attention to detail that goes into the manufacture of the Formula 1 cars they contain. There will be a couple of men employed solely to drive the trucks and generally help with stowing equipment, while the mechanics fly in on specially organised charter flights the day before first practice, and fly out again the night after the race. That way they can be back home and perhaps enjoy a well-earned day off on the Monday after a race before the transporter

Below *First day at the new circuit: world champion Alain Prost and his McLaren-TAG MP4/2C take a photocall, in August 1986, before the practice sessions at the Hungaroring for the first Hungarian Grand Prix since World War II. Drivers had to get to know every foot of the unfamiliar circuit as well as helping to put their cars into competitive trim for the race.*

Above *Alain Prost's McLaren-TAG on the tail lift of the team's transporter. The cars and equipment, and pit teams travel to and from circuits all over Europe in their vast trucks.*

arrives back at base on the Tuesday and preparation begins for the next race on the schedule.

PRACTICE DAYS

With Formula 1 practice and qualifying taking place on the Friday and Saturday prior to a grand prix, the transporters roll into the paddock on the Wednesday or Thursday. Before the cars can be readied for practice there is an enormous amount of hard work and detailed preparation to carry out, starting from the moment the transporter's huge rear doors drop down and the cars are rolled out into the pit lane garages.

The mechanics work as a well-drilled team. Top teams will have three men assigned to each car (the two nominated race cars and the spare). There will also be a gearbox specialist, technicians from the engine builder/supplier, an electrical expert, and a tyre fitter. While the cars are being unpacked with loving care, the tyre fitter will be taking the team's wheel rims to the tyre-supply truck to be fitted with the most suitable tyre for the job at that particular circuit.

Each mechanic has his own selection of tools: purpose-built trolleys, with all the tools on display, are wheeled to the front of the pit lane garage. Whatever tool is needed in a sudden mid-race crisis can be found in an instant.

Supplies of fuel are also kept at the back of the pit; air lines are connected to the high-speed

Right *Alain Prost, team boss Ron Dennis (rear, left) and other McLaren team members confer in the transporter during practice sessions for the 1986 Portuguese Grand Prix.*

power sockets for tightening or unscrewing the wheel-securing nuts. Inside the transporter a complete range of spares and accessories for each car is carried in purpose-built compartments; and once the cars have been unloaded, workbenches and power tools are available to create a self-contained mobile workshop capable of dealing with most technical disasters – short of a total write-off – during the grand-prix weekend.

On Friday morning the mechanics arrive early to complete the final detailed preparation of each car prior to the start of the first untimed practice session. By 8.00 am, two hours before the action begins, the cars will probably be ready, but right up to the moment they are rolled out on to the grid the mechanics will be fussing over them. If the weather is cold, radiator intakes will have been taped over so that the oil and water come up to working temperature as quickly as possible once the car starts running. If new brake pads, or perhaps a new gearbox, have been fitted the previous night, a note will be taped to the centre of the steering wheel, reminding the driver to take things carefully for the first few laps.

Then, of course, there are the spare parts: not only wheels and tyres, but spare wings, and a selection of nose sections painted with the correct race numbers. In an emergency, everybody knows what to do in a flash. Life in the pits may look fairly casual during untimed practice, but if quick action is needed – to change damaged bodywork, or to fit a new rear wing or a fresh set of tyres a few minutes before the end of the qualifying period, the mechanics spring into action with electrifying efficiency.

On the Saturday night before the race most teams will strip down their cars completely and fit freshly rebuilt engines. Then, on the Sunday morning, the relentless countdown to the race begins. There is an almost palpable tension among the mechanics as the cars edge out on to the track for the half-hour warm-up session. If

Right *Practice days in the pits: two engineers from the Honda factory at work on the engine of Nelson Piquet's Williams-Honda FW11 in preparation for qualifying sessions for the 1986 Italian Grand Prix at Monza. Honda-engined cars proved to be comfortably the fastest here, Piquet and Mansell taking first and second places in the race.*

HONDA
F-1
RACING TEAM
ICI
Miti
NGK
SPARK PLUGS
ROVER

there is a major problem now, things will be tight: an engine failure at this late stage can be a major drama. A well-drilled team could change an engine in the time available, but it would be a mammoth undertaking. If it has to be done, the mechanics from all three cars will muck in together to complete the task as quickly and efficiently as possible. Meanwhile, the spare car will be receiving an extra polish, its fuel tank topped up and a set of race tyres fitted – just in case it's going to be needed.

As the cars line up on the grid, the mechanics tending the spare car can afford to relax a bit. It looks as though their car can now be pushed back to the garage, pumped dry of its fuel load and prepared for loading into the transporter. But even when the red light gives way to the green and the pack is sprinting towards the first corner, their work may not be over. In the 1986 British Grand Prix, a multiple pile-up on the first corner resulted in the race being red-flagged to a halt after only one lap. By this time, Nigel Mansell's Williams had suffered a driveshaft breakage and was coasting slowly at the back of the field, the Englishman believing his chances to be over. Stopping and restarting the race gave him a tremendous second chance. However, there was no way in which the driveshaft could be changed in the time available, so the Williams mechanics rolled out the spare car to take its place, confident in the knowledge it was fully race-worthy in every respect. Mansell happily changed cars – and went on to score a momentous victory in front of a delighted home crowd.

Below *Ayrton Senna's Lotus-Honda having its one-piece body panel lowered into position in the pits before the 1987 San Marino Grand Prix at Imola.*

Left Nigel Mansell in a last-minute conference before a 1986 practice session.

26
GITANES
olivetti
COURTAULDS
COURTAULDS
ac monoceram
USF&G
West
West

THE RACE

During a race, it is best to keep away from the pits unless your presence is absolutely essential. The pit lane is part of the racing circuit and, in these days of routine pit stops to change tyres, racing cars usually enter it at racing speeds.

Two laps or so before a car is going to make a tyre stop, the mechanics are ready and waiting. They will have already laid a distinctive trail of coloured tape right up to the exact point in the pit lane where the car is to stop. At the back of the pit garages the replacement tyres are being heated in their tailor-made 'electric blankets'. Tyres naturally generate considerable heat in a race, so the manufacturers make tyres that operate most efficiently at racing temperature. The blankets heat the tyres to the required temperature, so that the driver does not have to waste time warming them up on the circuit. From the pit exit, or at least within a few hundred yards of it, he should be able to 'lean' on his tyres as hard as he likes!

Suddenly the moment has arrived! 'Their man' – Prost, Piquet, Mansell, Senna or whoever – hurtles into the pit lane and brakes to a halt, perfectly in position. The air is split with the metallic whirring of the wheel-locking sockets. Old wheels off: new wheels on: more whirring. The chief mechanic, standing at the front of the car facing the driver, waits until his colleagues at all four corners signify they have finished their task by leaping upright and raising one hand above the head. Then the chief mechanic signals the driver back into the race with a wave of his arm – and the car is gone almost before you have taken in the fact that all four wheels have been changed. At best, the car has been stationary for only seven or eight seconds!

For the winning mechanics, of course, there is the celebration and feeling of sheer elation at

Left *On the grid before the warm-up lap for the 1986 Hungarian Grand Prix. At top right is Senna (Lotus-Renault 98T); at top left is Piquet (Williams-Honda FW11), with team-mate Mansell behind him; Prost (McLaren-TAG MP4/2C) is behind Senna. Back-markers are, at right, Huub Rothengatter (Zakspeed 861) and, at left and last of all, Allen Berg (Osella-Alfa Romeo FA1F).*

Above *and* ***right*** *Two of the supreme 'quick-change' artists on the F1 scene go about their business during the 1987 season. In the picture above, Prost's McLaren pit team; on the right Senna's Lotus team. When on reasonable form, both teams can expect to change the tyres and signal the cars on their way in between seven and eight seconds; the Williams pit work is similarly spritely.*

being involved with a group of men who have 'got the job done'. But others are less lucky. Accident damage or mechanical failure may have claimed their machines during the course of a race. Perhaps the driver has crashed, in a split second putting at naught all that loving attention lavished on the car over the past ten days or so. It may now lie, bent and buckled, somewhere out on the circuit. Being a race mechanic calls for an enormous amount of resilience in situations like this!

Short-wave radio communication between car and team personnel have made life much easier for the grand-prix mechanic. Until a few years ago, conversation in the pit lane was limited to yells and erratic hand signals: precious little could be heard above the noise of the exhausts. Now the drivers, engineers and mechanics can be seen wearing head sets, calmly discussing practice problems with the minimum of fuss and drama.

With the emphasis on fuel economy in current Formula 1, sometimes apparently minor problems crop up during a race which do not even require the car to stop, but nonetheless demand

Left *The Williams pit team signals to Nigel Mansell during a 1986 race with information about rival Ayrton Senna and team-mate Nelson Piquet.*

a close liaison between engineers and drivers.

One of the most remarkable examples of F1 teamwork seen in recent years occurred during the 1987 Belgian Grand Prix at Spa-Franscorchamps and involved the McLaren team. Having an unusually easy time at the head of the field on his way to his 27th grand-prix triumph, Alain Prost was faced with a problem in the cockpit shortly after a typically slick McLaren pit stop for fresh tyres. The digital read-out on the instrument panel of the McLaren suddenly stopped working. All Alain was left with was a rev counter. Deep in the computerised ignition/fuel system, a tiny plug had come out of its socket. There was nothing wrong with the car, but Prost now lacked vital information: he needed to know about his fuel situation – how much he was using and how much he had left. When the plug came adrift, a 'fail-safe' system on the TAG turbo engine automatically adjusted itself to a preprogrammed turbo-boost setting that was different from that at which Prost had been running. Even though he was under no real pressure from his rivals at the time, Prost nonetheless needed the computer's on-going read-out so that he would know the extent to which he would be able to respond to a challenge to his lead without running out of fuel.

Prost spoke to his engineer on his radio link and explained the problem. There was no panic: the pit crew simply got into radio contact with Prost's team-mate Stefan Johansson, who was running second in the other McLaren, and asked him to read out his own (quite satisfactory) fuel-consumption figure. This was relayed to Prost – and he sped on to victory without the slightest further hitch. Nobody would have known about the drama if Prost himself had not mentioned it, almost casually, after the race.

Despite the presence of such electronic gadgetry, the mechanics may well be called upon to

Below Mansell, like other F1 drivers, can communicate with his pit during a race by means of a radio link. The speaker and earphones are incorporated into his helmet. The black stick-like radio aerial can be seen on the nose of the car.

improvise in certain circumstances. They may have to tape up a driver's broken helmet visor at a panic pit stop, or struggle with a sticking rear-wheel nut, or clear radiator ducts of obstructive paper, or other detritus picked up from the track, which may be threatening to overheat the engine. Whatever the problem, top mechanics are drilled to cope with it methodically and without fuss. To the outsider it looks as though they are taking their time. But the old maxim 'more haste, less speed' applies more pointedly to motor racing than probably to any other high-tech sport.

In little more than an hour and a half the race is over. The winning driver climbs the victor's rostrum, acknowledges the cheers of the crowd by spraying champagne over their heads, and disappears from view. Then the mechanics get on with the business of clearing up the debris. Oil-stained racing cars and a pit garage full of scattered equipment take some gathering together. The hydraulic lift on the back of the articulated transporter is primed ready for use, the cars pumped dry of fuel, and the tyres stripped from their wheel rims for returning to the tyre-company's truck. The cars are given a rub over, checked for any obvious damage and then rolled, one by one, on to the ramp and lifted into the snug interior of the transporter.

Engines are crated up and stowed in their own special compartments between the wheels of the trailer unit, while specialised components are packed in dozens of drawers inside the truck. It is like packing a Chinese puzzle. Within three or four hours the doors are closed, the big diesel's

***Below** Michele Alboreto's Ferrari F187 makes a quick getaway after a tyre change. The Italian* équipe *is rarely as slick at this operation as the British teams.*

Above *Victory for Prost: the McLaren team jubilant as the world champion takes the flag in the 1986 Australian Grand Prix at Adelaide.*

engine booms into life amid a cloud of blue smoke, and the 'big rigs' begin rumbling out of the paddock, headlights picking out the litter and debris scattered across the paddock floor after a day at the races. Ten days later, at some other venue across Europe – or on the other side of the world – the whole complex process of preparing the cars in the pit lane will begin all over again.

This, then, is the mechanics' domain – a workplace staffed by shrewd, adept and committed men, who love machinery and guard their team's reputation and secrets with all the enthusiasm and professionalism displayed by their top-line drivers. The pit lane is a private world with its own conventions, its own gossip, its own procedures. At the end of the day, you can always get another driver. But the respected chief mechanic in the pit lane may well have 20 years' experience under his belt. If he is good, he will be in great demand.

ICI
BOSS
Nigel Mansell

THE RACE

HOT, STICKY, EXCITING!

BRAZILIAN GRAND PRIX

A Boost for Frank Williams

The Brazilian Grand Prix, now firmly established as the opening round of the World Championship, is awaited eagerly by fans the world over. It is the end of the close season, which will have been dominated by rumours spread by the media, the launch of new cars, news of test sessions and the signing of drivers.

A fever of excitement surges through Formula 1 followers, most of them ready to swell a worldwide television audience running into seemingly uncountable millions. For Brazilian fans it is the showpiece when they hope a local driver will fend off all invaders. Emerson Fittipaldi won the World Championship for them on two occasions (1972, 1974), taking the Brazilian event in 1973 and 1974, while Nelson Piquet took the title in 1981 and 1983 and won in Brazil in the latter year. So there were plenty of grounds for optimism.

The crowds travelling the short distance down the coast from Río to the Jacarepagua track in 1986 had little interest in any driver but Piquet and Ayrton Senna. Fans were sharply divided about these local heroes, with comparatively new boy Ayrton perhaps getting more votes – the world always seems to love the underdog – but the Williams cars of Piquet and Britain's Nigel Mansell were in promising form after wins at the end of 1985.

This is a grand prix which some journalists and broadcasters try to avoid. It's great to be in at the start of the championship battle, but the heat and humidity, plus the ever-present chance of getting mugged, makes it a difficult assignment. Several of the European contingent, including a British driver, have been attacked in Río. It is a place where women, if they are wise, do not carry easily nicked handbags, and where one photographer camouflages his equipment in a supermarket bag and stuffs his money and credit cards down his socks.

There is no denying, though, that there is a real atmosphere at the circuit, which is set back a little from the ocean and with most of the crowd massed in huge grandstands along the main straight. The crowds arrive early, scrambling for good vantage points, while a thoughtful fire-brigade hoses them down from time to time in the sticky heat.

For British fans there was one face missing. A few days earlier Frank Williams, boss of the Williams team, had met with a horrific road accident and was lying almost completely paralysed in a London hospital. He still managed to retain contact with his team, however, while they did all they could to keep his spirits up.

Before the race began, with Senna on pole in his

TYRRELL ON JACAREPAGUA

The chief problem for the teams is that they arrive from a European winter and are thrown overnight into tremendous heat and humidity. As to the track, its surface is very abrasive, which means that the higher-powered cars have to change tyres at least twice. But new tyres, when warmed up, produce a considerable advantage, so that a driver can soon pull back time lost in the pits. The drivers have an additional problem: there is great strain on neck muscles through two very long left-hand corners. This is particularly evident if they haven't been to Río for pre-season testing, since they will not have been using these muscles during the close season.

Pages 124–5 *Nigel Mansell in the Williams-Honda FW11 in which he took second place in the 1986 Formula 1 drivers' championship, two points behind Alain Prost and one ahead of his teammate Nelson Piquet.*

Below, left *Veteran team boss Ken Tyrrell, who comments on each of the Formula 1 circuits. Tyrrell has won two constructors' titles (1969 and 1971), and Jackie Stewart won his three drivers' titles with the Tyrrell team.*

Below *The start of the 1986 Brazilian Grand Prix. Ayrton Senna in the Lotus-Renault 98T (12) leads Nigel Mansell and Nelson Piquet in Williams-Honda FW11s (5 and 6). Michele Alboreto in the Ferrari F156/85 (27) is at left; René Arnoux in the Ligier-Renault JS27 (25) is behind Senna.*

black and gold Lotus, Piquet alongside him on the front row and Nigel Mansell just behind in the other Williams, the whole GP circus got together before the TV cameras to give Frank Williams an uplift. Ranged around Piquet's car they held up a banner reading, 'Don't worry Frank – we are minding the store'.

In splendid form, with his Honda-powered Williams clearly the quickest car, Piquet gave Frank and his home fans a real treat. He got the measure of Senna after two laps and lost the lead only briefly during two planned pit stops for tyres. This is the circuit which eats tyres faster than any other.

Senna could do nothing to thwart his compatriot and had to be content with second place in his Lotus. The Honda engineers had done a fine job in organising their engine-management system to provide just the right balance between power and fuel consumption, since no-one could start with more than 195 litres (43 gallons) aboard. The Renault engine in Senna's Lotus might match it for power but was thirstier, so Senna had to be resigned to keeping down his turbocharger boost and settling for second place.

The only driver to offer any challenge to Piquet was world champion Alain Prost, whose McLaren in race trim had been fastest in the morning warm-up. But his TAG engine failed at half distance; and the same thing had happened to his new team-mate Keke Rosberg early on.

Although most of the spectators would not agree, this was not the greatest of races. But it did provide early excitement when Mansell, anxious to grab the lead, tangled with Senna and slid into the barrier and retirement. This was the second time in successive years that Mansell had put himself out in a first-lap fracas. If he had waited a while he could well have picked up the points which would have given him the World Championship later on. But motor racing is crammed with ifs, and the massed crowd could hardly care less as Piquet and Senna got together on the podium to wave the Brazilian flag.

Back in his hospital bed, Frank Williams was soon watching a video recording of the race which had been hastened round to him from an understanding BBC. It must have done him a lot of good.

Main picture *Nelson Piquet on lap 19 makes the first of his two pit stops for new tyres. For this opening race of the season, the Williams-Honda clearly had the best speed-economy mix of the main contenders.*

Inset *Winner Piquet with runner-up Senna (left) and third-placed Jacques Laffite. The race was a minor triumph for the Ligier team, Laffite being followed into fourth place by team-mate René Arnoux.*

WELCOME TO ANDALUCIA!

A Nail-Biting Finish

The Spanish Grand Prix has had a somewhat chequered history. In the last two decades it has fluctuated between the Jarama circuit, outside Madrid, and the dramatic but dangerous Montjuich track set in a Barcelona park. The 1975 Grand Prix at Montjuich was a disaster, with a multiple crash and the race later halted after the leading car leapt a barrier and killed four bystanders.

Five years later the race at Jarama saw a bitter struggle for power between the sport's ruling body and the constructors' association, which resulted in a reduced field and the event being ruled out of the World Championship. After the 1981 race (again at Jarama) the Spanish Grand Prix disappeared from the calendar until 1986, when it resumed at a new circuit built in record time a little way outside Jerez, the heart of the sherry industry in south-west Spain.

A lot of local pesetas had been thrown into producing a good-looking track with numerous well-sited viewing areas; but sadly, from the organisers' point of view, it was a flop. The sherry firms are comfortably off, but most of the local population is far from rich. Admission charges had clearly been set too high, and despite the new attraction many thousands stayed at home to watch the race on TV. The bare stands, looking from the air like gigantic solar cells, bore witness to this.

Ayrton Senna made a bit of history in qualifying, giving Lotus their hundredth pole position, while Martin Brundle blotted his copybook by crashing Ken Tyrrell's new 015 on the eve of the race.

If the crowd was a disappointment, the race certainly was not. Held under a blue sky but in chilly conditions, it looked at first like being something of a procession. Senna led with Piquet's Williams behind and it looked as though the two Brazilians would reverse the top finishing order of the previous championship round.

Then Nigel Mansell began to make a charge. Spectators cannot know the whole story as a race unfolds. The reason for Mansell's prudent driving in the early stages was known only to the driver and his team: his on-board computer was telling him he was using more fuel than he should be; if he turned up his turbocharger boost he risked using up his 195 litres of fuel before the finish. When his cockpit read-out suggested he could at last press on without running out of petrol he did just that.

Shortly before half distance Mansell had stormed through into second place and a few laps later he was in front. With Piquet out of the hunt with engine trouble it was looking like a two-horse race; though the calculating Prost was playing a waiting game, no doubt hoping that the pace-setters would overstrain their cars or make crucial driving errors under the stress of bitter competition.

The factor which decided the result and brought a thrilling finish was tyre wear. The Goodyear technicians had calculated that the leading cars

Left *Martin Brundle's brand new Tyrrell-Renault 015 skidded off the track and into the armco during qualifying on the Saturday, finishing up by the hospitality units near the final corner of the circuit. He had to drive one of the older 014 cars in the race retiring after 41 laps with oil-system failure.*

Below *The start at Jerez: Ayrton Senna, in pole position again, is disappearing at left, followed by Nelson Piquet (centre) and Nigel Mansell. Keke Rosberg (McLaren-TAG MP4/ 2C) is behind Piquet, and his McLaren team-mate Alain Prost tails Mansell. Of these five only Piquet retired, the others filling the first four places.*

TYRRELL ON JEREZ

The circuit was brand new for 1986, with excellent facilities and up-to-date pits which, from a team manager's point of view, is always important. It calls for a very well-balanced car because it has numerous corners and not much of a straight. It is the sort of a circuit where a well set-up car will always do well. There are few opportunities for overtaking; really only on the pits straight – and even that follows a relatively slow corner. Since all the cars go round slow corners at the same speed, it is very difficult to develop a passing manoeuvre.

Above Senna's Lotus-Renault 98T in the pit before the race. No one could be certain how the race tyres would fare on the brand-new circuit. Senna completed the race without a tyre change; Prost, who came third, reckoned he would have won if he had changed tyres at about two-thirds of the distance.

would complete the race without a tyre change. Indeed, Senna did just that, though his tyres were balanced on the edge of disaster by the finish. Mansell's tyres, however, were clearly deteriorating, affecting his car's performance. With 10 laps to go Senna was back in the lead after forcing his way past Mansell on the inside at the uphill hairpin.

Knowing he could not match Senna on his worn tyres, Mansell roared into the pits for a very fast change. Out again, he was now third, behind Prost, and seemingly incapable of getting back the lead. He was 20 seconds behind Senna with nine laps left. It looked an impossible task – but those new tyres, once they had warmed to operating temperature, rejuvenated Mansell's performance.

Mansell's computer showed him he could turn up the boost without running out of fuel. Now he was flying, but he still had to overtake Prost, a difficult task on this circuit. Prost was not making it easy, fending off Mansell by cramming on the boost on the pits straight with four laps to go. Mansell did get by Prost later on that lap and began to overhaul Senna relentlessly – but the effort had cost him vital fractions of a second.

With two laps to go the gap was down to 4.6 seconds. As the leaders went into the last lap, with everyone on their toes with excitement, Mansell was only 1.5 seconds behind. It was one of the most gripping final grand-prix laps of recent years, and as the pair went into the last left-hander Mansell took advantage of the Williams' superior braking to get right on Senna's tail.

Senna saw the threat, jinked one way and then the other but could not prevent Mansell drawing ever closer. As they crossed the line Mansell thought he had won; he had to see the video replay before he was convinced. In fact he had lost by a mere 14 hundredths of a second. It was the closest finish since Peter Gethin pinched the 1971 Italian Grand Prix for BRM from Ronnie Peterson's March.

With hindsight it was evident that this was a race Mansell could have won if he had changed tyres one or two laps earlier. Indeed, it was later agreed that any one of the three front runners, by switching to new rubber for, say, the last 20 laps, would have been assured of victory.

Right *Senna (left) beats Mansell to the flag in the closest finish to a Formula 1 race for 15 years. The winning margin was 0.014 sec – a few inches after 188 miles!*

FERRARI'S HOME GROUND

SAN MARINO GRAND PRIX

The Professor Cuts It Fine

Below *Getting the cars into position on the grid before the start at Imola. The San Marino race proved to be a test for the cars' fuel-consumption computers and the drivers' ability to go strictly according to the read-outs. Prost, as expected, proved a master at this particular game, shading Piquet by about 11 seconds.*

Below, right *Alessandro Nannini (Minardi-Motori Moderni M185B) had no need to worry about fuel consumption: he came to grief at the first corner after bumping Laffite's Ligier-Renault JS27.*

One of the oddities, some would say injustices, of grand-prix racing is that Britain, with the strongest spectator following of all, has only a single World Championship race while Italy, albeit also with hordes of fans, hosts two.

The Italians have their own grand prix at Monza and another called the San Marino Grand Prix. This latter race is not, in fact, held in the small independent republic 10 miles south-west of Rimini but at Imola, some 45 miles up the Autostrada del Sol towards Bologna. San Marino is very happy to get publicity for its 38 square miles as a tourist attraction, while the Italians are more than pleased to have two grands prix a year on their territory.

The Imola circuit, on the outskirts of a town packed with ancient buildings and some good restaurants, had a major rebuild in 1980 and staged the Italian Grand Prix that year, before the race went back to its traditional home at Monza. Since 1981 Imola has been the venue of the San Marino Grand Prix.

Enzo Ferrari is said to have had a hand in planning the track, which is named after his late son, Dino. It is a fine circuit, tough on both drivers and cars, with gradients to provide both interest and challenge. It has one main drawback for spectators: the enormous traffic jams that develop in the area after the race is over.

There are splendid vantage points for the *tifosi* (the race-crazy Italian fans), and with Maranello not far away most of them are always rooting for Ferrari. Indeed, they have little interest in any other cars and their delight when one of their favourite blood-red machines gains an advantage – even if it is only to move from sixth to fifth – is deafening.

Imola is tough on fuel consumption. With tank capacity limited to 195 litres, the 1986 teams had to find that delicate balance between engine power and thirst. A no-hoper looking for brief glory could give his engine maximum turbo-charger boost and head the field for a while – but a dry tank would find him out well before the end. Drivers had, in fact, run out of fuel in the 1985 Grand Prix and it was to happen again in 1986.

Purists argue that this is not real racing, more an economy run; and there is some truth in that. But if grand-prix racing is to reflect the pinnacle of technical engineering excellence, this fuel-capacity rule certainly puts the emphasis on the skill of the engineers as well as on the cool-headedness of the men in the cockpit.

At Imola in 1986 it was the canny Alain Prost, not known as the Professor for nothing, who played the fuel game impeccably – though even he only just managed to persuade his McLaren across the line with an empty tank.

In 1985 Prost had run out of fuel at Imola shortly after taking the chequered flag; but he was later disqualified when his car was declared to be fractionally underweight. In 1986, Prost's McLaren began to cough and splutter on the final lap as his fuel drained low. The Frenchman stayed cool. He flicked his steering wheel abruptly one way and then the other to coax the remaining dregs of petrol to the TAG engine, while his car described a violently serpentine path. The car went slower and slower and the crowd roared as Nelson Piquet, who had probably pressed too hard when he led at the beginning but had got back to the required consumption level through easing off, was rapidly overhauling the leader. The chase failed, by less than eight seconds, and Prost coasted across the line, a very relieved driver, for his first win of the season.

Prost's team-mate, Keke Rosberg, was less fortunate in the economy run; he parked, out of fuel, with less than two laps to go, complaining that he had lost what had looked like certain second place because his gauge provided duff information. Riccardo Patrese also ran dry on the same lap, robbed of fourth place, but he still earned a point for sixth best.

The Imola circuit is also extremely tough on brakes, as Stefan Johansson found to his cost. The crowd groaned their disappointment as the Ferrari driver was forced to give way to Gerhard Berger's Benetton and had to be content with fourth place at the finish.

There had been further disappointment for the *tifosi* when Michele Alboreto brought his Ferrari into the pits to retire. Though the reason was officially given as 'loss of boost pressure' there were suspicions that he, too, had driven an over-thirsty race.

Berger was another driver who used his head. He drove the last 30 laps without a clutch and demonstrated fine presence of mind in the dying yards of the race when, lying third, he could have unlapped himself by passing the struggling Prost. He summed up the situation immediately, let Prost cross the line ahead of him and so saved himself doing a further lap which he might not have completed. This was the first time the young Austrian had been on a grand-prix podium. It was a foretaste of even better things to come later in the season.

Right *Ayrton Senna's Imola race was brief: here smoke pours from the Lotus-Renault shortly before he retired with wheel-bearing failure after 11 laps.*

TYRRELL ON IMOLA

This is a particularly interesting circuit. There is a long straight with a slow corner at the end of it which brings out the very worst in braking problems. It is a circuit which is very, very hard on brakes and also very heavy on fuel, as witness the number of cars which have run dry there. The facilities are really excellent and it is a very well-run motor race.

Below *Alain Prost (right), tank almost dry, totters past the chequered flag while Gerhard Berger (Benetton-BMW B186), safely in third place, keeps behind him to avoid having to do another lap.*

POSEURS' PARADISE

MONACO GRAND PRIX

Hat-trick for Prost

Below *The first four on the grid – Prost, Senna, Mansell, and Michele Alboreto (Ferrari F186) – go into the first corner, Ste-Dévote, before the climb up to Massenet corner and Casino square.*

Right *Mansell illuminations: sparks fly as the Williams bottoms out while emerging from the tunnel. Mansell took fourth place in spite of his ailing engine's sluggish acceleration out of Monaco's many slow corners.*

Of all the races in the championship calendar the Monaco Grand Prix is the one which attracts the greatest world-wide attention, which the most fans want to attend and which is given most media coverage. The reasons are obvious: the setting oozes with 24-carat glamour. Monte Carlo is packed with beautiful people, the fabulous yachts of the rich bob up and down in the harbour, in the narrow streets your every-day 911 Carreras give way to Testa Rossas and Countachs, and for a few days the less rich can feel they are rubbing shoulders with the famous and plutocratic. It is a royal occasion, too, with Prince Rainier or members of his family coming down from the fairytale palace of the Grimaldis on the hill to watch from a flag-bedecked tribune.

No wonder a well-known British travel firm flies in thousands of spectators each year. Not surprising, either, that the hotels charge outrageously exorbitant prices; and they are abetted by a programme which traditionally starts with practice a day early, with Friday a rest day, enabling the locals to make even more of a killing from visitors.

The sponsors love the race for the quality of exposure it provides. Even for sponsors, though, it can be fraught. For many years the grid has been restricted on the grounds of safety: race traffic is heavy on the narrow, twisty circuit, which winds through the streets, under a tunnel leading back to the harbour, and around the large swimming pool by the harbour-side. Every year some teams have to pack up their bags and leave after the practice sessions, having failed to make the grid, their sponsors sick as a *perroquet*. (Imagine how the backers of the McLaren team felt in 1983 when both Niki Lauda and John Watson were in trouble on the first day of practice and had no chance of qualifying when it rained on the final qualifying day.)

The teams, and especially the drivers, have less affection for the Monaco Grand Prix. Working conditions in the makeshift pits are necessarily poor and the drivers know that this event can be as much of a lottery as placing bets in the ornate Casino. Yet this is one race which drivers desperately want to win, to prove themselves in front of a huge global audience. They may not like it, but they grit their teeth and get on with the job, hoping for the breaks and trusting that the wheel-cracking kerbs of the city streets will not catch them out or a slick of oil send them hurtling into the unrelenting Armco. With only 20 on the grid there were six sidelined drivers in 1986, five of them the expected tail-end runners but including Johnny Dumfries (Lotus) who had a load of traumas during practice.

Monte Carlo does not always have fine weather in May. There have been several occasions recently when rain has influenced the outcome. But on race day in 1986 the weather was sunny and benign. Alain Prost, winner in the two previous years, was out for a hat-trick. He achieved just that, with a display of precision driving that stamped him as the master of this treacherous course, where the slightest error can bring disaster.

In his red and white McLaren the World Champion dominated the race as he had dominated qualifying. He lost the lead for only a few laps when Ayrton Senna slipped by while he called in for fresh tyres; but he regained it when Senna did the same. McLaren team-mate Keke Rosberg also got the measure of Senna to relegate the Brazilian to third at the finish. Fourth place went to Mansell, who had one of the most exhausting races of his career, struggling with sudden power surge out of the slow corners. He was not the only sufferer. The Monaco circuit calls for hundreds of gear-changes in a race of just over 160 miles, leaving the gear-change hand like a lump of raw meat. Stefan Johansson's right hand was in an awful state, since the top of his Ferrari gear lever broke right off, leaving the Swede with only a few inches of jagged metal with which to change ratios. He was classified tenth but it was a miracle he finished at all.

The 1986 race was, as so often at Monaco, something of a procession, enlivened only by an exciting battle for eighth place between Patrick Tambay's Lola-Ford and Martin Brundle's Tyrrell-Renault which could so nearly have ended in tragedy.

As Brundle turned into the Mirabeau right-hander just after the Casino the French driver tried to overtake on the inside. There was contact and the Lola went into a dramatic aerial roll, rammed the guard rail and fortunately landed back on its wheels. Brundle went on but broke down before he got back to the pits. But he carried a sinister memento of the accident – a tyre mark on his helmet which showed just how close he had been to disaster.

Not a great race, then, except for those aficionados able to appreciate a Prost demonstration of the highest quality.

Above *The 'law' of Monaco says that back-markers on the grid haven't a chance, owing to the difficulty of overtaking. Keke Rosberg did his best to give the lie to that, starting in ninth position and working his way through the field to finish second to his McLaren team-mate Prost. It was to be the closest Rosberg came to victory in his last season in Formula 1.*

TYRRELL ON MONACO

From the teams' point of view, Monaco is a nightmare. It has no permanent facilities and every day we have to move several tons of equipment to the pits from the paddock alongside the harbour. And there is no shelter if it rains. It is really primitive for the teams. But it is the glamour race of the year because of the setting, and it is always a very hard fought race. It is very difficult for the drivers because there is no respite, no straight for them to take a breather: they have to concentrate hard the whole time. Opportunities for overtaking are very few indeed. In fact, with cars doing similar lap times there is no chance at all, unless a driver makes a mistake or gets baulked by a much slower car in a difficult place and offers his pursuer a momentary advantage.

Right *Winner Prost comes out of Tabac corner pursued by Michele Alboreto (Ferrari F186), Thierry Boutsen (Arrows-BMW A8), Keke Rosberg, and Stefan Johansson (Ferrari F186). Prost's winning margin was a very comfortable 24 seconds.*

SPA – DRIVERS' FAVOURITE

BELGIAN GRAND PRIX

Mansell Majestic

Talk to Formula 1 drivers and you will discover that almost without exception they are agreed that the Spa-Francorchamps circuit is their favourite. It has virtually everything to provide the challenge which they relish. There are flat-out sections where speeds approach 200 miles an hour, gradients to provide interest, high-speed corners that call for fine judgement and precision, and a hairpin which regularly catches out those who brake too late.

The current circuit, using public roads in the pine-clad Ardennes south-east of Liège, is a shortened version of the fantastically fast track where, in 1970, Pedro Rodriguez in a BRM pipped Chris Amon's March to the line by just over a second at fractionally under 150 miles an hour. That was the last time the 8.75-mile circuit staged a grand prix. It was clearly becoming too dangerous; fatalities had scarred its history and there were fears for spectator safety as well.

Thirteen years later the Belgian Grand Prix returned to a revised circuit, halved in length and cutting out the daunting Burnenville corner, the high-speed Masta straight which seemed to go on for ever, and the difficult Stavelot sweep at the end of it. The architects had done a great job, joining up the first and last parts of the old circuit with a downhill section incorporating a series of fast corners well calculated to challenge the world's top drivers. It was just what was needed to please drivers anxious to prove their worth and spectators relishing the sight of Formula 1 cars teetering on the very brink of adhesion.

The pits on the old circuit were on a downhill straight leading to the impressive Eau Rouge corner. They are still there but are now used for other races: new pits have been built on a level stretch just before La Source hairpin that leads to the old pits area. The only drawback to this is that the main grandstands are still opposite the old pits, so that spectators there cannot see what is happening when cars come into the new pits for tyre changes or repairs. When there is no racing the circuit is open to the public, and it includes a bus-stop positioned close to the pits which forms a chicane.

The revised circuit certainly retains the flavour of the old and the only feature that calls for real criticism is that the starting grid is too close to La

Above *The shunt at the first corner at Spa. Prost, crowded by the line taken by both Senna and Berger, knocked off his nose cone when tangling with Berger's Benetton-BMW B186. In the picture, Prost and Berger are at right; Senna (centre), Alboreto (left) and Mansell are unscathed; Piquet has already cleared the corner.*

Left *An aerial view of the starting grid at Spa-Francorchamps. The first-corner accident occurred at the hairpin at the extreme left of the picture.*

TYRRELL ON SPA

This is a wonderful circuit. It is great for spectators who can watch the cars through all those beautiful curves at the far end of the circuit; and there are excellent facilities for the teams in the new pits. It is exactly the opposite of Monaco, with plenty of overtaking opportunities. It is an 'engine circuit' where you really need a powerful car, and because engines are used particularly hard it is very tough on them.

Right *Nigel Mansell leads Stefan Johansson (Ferrari F186); sparks fly from the Lotus-Renault 98T of Johnny Dumfries. Mansell impressively won his speed versus fuel economy duel with the pursuing Ayrton Senna, eventually winning by a comfortable margin. Prost, after his first-corner fracas, drove magnificently, recorded the fastest lap, and finished sixth.*

Source hairpin. It was this that caused mayhem in the 1986 Grand Prix as the pack battled for an early advantage. In the melée that arose when too many cars tried to use the same bit of road, Patrick Tambay's Lola crashed into retirement and Alain Prost knocked the nose cone off his McLaren. Prost had to come in for repairs, losing almost a whole lap, before beginning a magnificent drive which brought him the consolation of sixth place and a single championship point.

The year before, Ayrton Senna had driven his Lotus to victory ahead of Nigel Mansell. This time it was Nigel's turn for revenge – though not without drama. Mansell's Williams team-mate, Nelson Piquet, had looked like romping away with the race until his engine blew, while Mansell had lost time when he braked too late going into the bus-stop chicane; his car bounced over the kerb and spun wildly, but he managed to recover and continue the race in fourth place.

Senna took over the lead when Piquet went out and Mansell got up to second place. Mansell swooped into the pits for a typically fast Williams pit stop of just under eight seconds, and on fresh tyres he soon took the lead, which he held to the finish.

Everyone had wondered whether Senna would be able to pull out the stops and challenge Mansell; both drivers were anxiously watching their fuel read-outs, worried that giving their engines extra boost would see them stranded before 43 laps were completed. But the Renault engine in Senna's Lotus was shown still to be less frugal than Mansell's Honda, and this time he had to give best to the Williams driver. In the Williams pits, designer Patrick Head was constantly telling Mansell through radio contact to keep a close eye on his fuel, but the Englishman played it to perfection. At the end neither Mansell nor Senna could have driven another lap without running dry.

This was the third grand prix win of Mansell's career, with the clear promise of more to come. And in the post-race celebrations it was a thoughtful Mansell, both happy and sad, who dedicated his victory to Elio de Angelis, his former team-mate and good friend at Lotus, who had lost his life in a testing accident in France only a few days earlier.

Below *Mansell, Senna (left) and Johansson celebrate. Johansson's third place and team-mate Michele Alboreto's fourth were encouraging for the Ferrari team, whose cars managed comfortably on the fuel allowance.*

ROUND AND ROUND THE ISLAND

CANADIAN GRAND PRIX

Nigel Heads the Gang of Five

Opposite page *Ferrari conference: Michele Alboreto and (at rear) Stefan Johansson during practice sessions at Montreal. The Ferraris were plagued by turbo problems before the race.*

Left *Early exit: Patrick Tambay walks away from his Lola-Ford THL2 after the car went out of control and crashed at the first corner on the warm-up lap.*

I little thought when I visited Montreal prior to the opening of Expo '67 that I would be back to watch grand prix racing there just over a decade later. The Montreal circuit is on a man-made island in the St Lawrence Seaway. It was originally called after the name of the island, Île Nôtre-Dame, but after the death of the brilliant French-Canadian driver Gilles Villeneuve it was renamed in his memory. The island retains exhibition halls from Expo '67; it has a further claim to fame, for it includes a straight stretch of water where the rowing Olympics were staged in 1976. The press complex comprises what used to be the Olympic changing rooms.

There is a good atmosphere at the circuit and in Montreal itself (the largest French-speaking city in the world after Paris), and there are restaurants of high quality, particularly in the old part of the city. All in all, a good environment for holding a grand prix, although the teams are fiercely tested by the twin problems of high fuel-consumption and heavy strain on brakes.

The inaugural grand prix in Montreal in 1978 could not have been better scripted to satisfy the Quebeçois fans, for local hero Gilles Villeneuve drove his Ferrari to the first of six wins during an all-too-brief career (which ended tragically during final practice for the 1982 Belgian Grand Prix at Zolder). The crowds rolled up in their thousands the following year, hoping for a repeat performance by Villeneuve. This time, however, he had to give best to Alan Jones in a Williams after a memorable duel which lasted for the whole race. This was one occasion when the TV producers could be forgiven for concentrating almost entirely on the leaders. Villeneuve's Ferrari led for the first 50 laps of the 72-lap race, but was always dogged by Jones who had started alongside his rival on the front row of the grid. Then on lap 51 came the vital break when Jones got inside the Ferrari under braking for the hairpin before the pits. The two cars banged wheels but Jones was through and now it was his turn to be harried. But the Australian held on to win a classic battle by just over a second.

For the 1986 event Nigel Mansell, fresh from his success in Belgium, went to Montreal brimming over with confidence – this despite the fact that for him it was not a circuit with the happiest of memories, for he had had accidents there in 1981 and 1982. This time, though, it would be very different.

TYRRELL ON MONTREAL

I think it's a wonderful idea holding a grand prix on an island where there is no public car parking. The crowds all walk over from another nearby island, leaving their cars there or arriving by Metro. From the team's point of view it is like Monte Carlo, with the paddock a quarter of a mile away from the pits and no shelter in the pits at all. It is a circuit very heavy on fuel – probably the thirstiest in the calendar – and also very hard on brakes. It offers the drivers several challenges, particularly the fast corner after the pits. The one serious design fault is that this corner is too close to the pits exit, which can make for dangerous situations.

He stamped his authority over all concerned by snatching pole position on the grid from Senna's Lotus in qualifying, and was even more dominant in the race. Admittedly Keke Rosberg pushed his McLaren into the lead for a few laps, but that was while Mansell was keeping a very watchful eye on the fuel gauge and tempering his combative instinct with an engineer's practicality. It was not long before Mansell decided he could turn up the turbo boost and take over again. Apart from one lap, when he lost first place to Alain Prost while in the pits for fresh tyres, he sailed home well clear of the world champion for his second victory in succession. Mansell made it look all too simple. Indeed, he did find it an easy victory: at one point he radioed his team to tell them things were becoming boring out on the track and to enquire if anything exciting was happening in the pits!

The 1986 season seemed to be becoming the property of what Ken Tyrrell dubbed the Gang of Five: the Williams drivers Mansell and Piquet, the McLaren-mounted Prost and Rosberg, with Senna making up the number for Lotus. In 1986 at Montreal they filled the first five places; behind Mansell and Prost the order was Piquet, Rosberg and Senna.

There have been constant complaints about the siting of the pits exit at Montreal. It is sited between (and quite close to) a very fast section taken in top gear and a fast corner, and in 1986 the critics were unfortunately vindicated by what could have been a very serious accident. Johnny Dumfries came out of the pits in his Lotus after a tyre change just as Stefan Johansson's Ferrari was roaring by at high speed. The Swede had no chance of avoiding the Lotus and both drivers were put out of the race.

A pity, this, but nothing could detract from a splendid demonstration of dominance by Mansell, followed by the rest of the Gang.

Right *Nigel Mansell dominated the race after half way to take his second grand prix in succession. He won comfortably from Alain Prost (second) and team-mate Nelson Piquet, who had brake-related tyre problems.*

Below *During practice Teo Fabi (Benetton-BMW B186) crashed into the armco in the pit area and bounced across to the other side of the track, damaging both front and rear of his car.*

Canon
DENIM
Mobil 1
HONDA
ICI
Tactel
HONDA
Mobil
5
GOODYEAR

MOTOWN SPECTACULAR

Senna 'The Pole' Scorches Home

Detroit is a newcomer to the Formula 1 scene. The race grew out of a desire by the city fathers and bosses of the big car firms to burnish the darkened image of Motown, hit by recession and high unemployment, much of it run down and plagued by crime.

The grand prix circus first went to Detroit in 1982, and most of the drivers did not like what they saw. They found the track tortuous, featureless and dangerous. Jackie Stewart had done his best to hype the race in advance, suggesting it was the American answer to Monte Carlo; quite simply it lacked both the gradients and glamour of the principality.

Ken Tyrrell is perhaps a trifle biased: his team has shown up well there and in 1983 Michele Alboreto drove a Tyrrell to victory to give the legendary Ford-Cosworth V8 engine its 155th and final Formula 1 victory – the end of an astonishing story which began with debut success in the 1967 Dutch Grand Prix.

There used to be a rule (it still exists as far as I know) that any new circuit must stage a 'probationary' event to prove it has the organisation to run a Formula 1 race. That rule was overlooked before the 1982 Detroit Grand Prix, and some chaos resulted. The organisation has since been smartened up and minor changes have been made to the track, including smoothing over the many manhole covers which prompted angry driver criticism.

Despite the patchy quality of officialdom and the forbidding prices charged by hotels, Detroit has come through and has produced some exciting racing. The 1982 race was a real cracker. After the chaotic situation on the practice days and a dubious decision to re-start the race after a few laps, the event was distinguished by a classic drive still spoken of in bated breath by those who appreciate star quality.

It was in fact the stoppage of the race after seven laps, following a melée which by no means blocked the track, which led to a faultless performance from John Watson. The Ulsterman had hardly been impressive in practice, qualifying only 17th on the grid. While the track was being cleared ready for the restart his McLaren was fitted with harder-compound tyres which transformed the car's handling.

Below *Senna (Lotus-Renault 98T) flashes by the pit area well ahead of the field. In the background the new Renaissance Center rises above the drab shore area.*

Right *Jacques Laffite, having endured suspension problems on the bumpy Detroit circuit during practice, gave Team Ligier a tremendous boost by taking second place in the race.*

Watson was now in fantastic form, slicing through the field with incisive moves that staggered his rivals. On a track with so few places for overtaking he achieved the seemingly impossible, and a little over half way through the race he was in the lead, ahead even of his team-mate, Niki Lauda (who later made an uncharacteristic mistake to crash out of the race). It was a memorable performance, and after coming third in Detroit the following year (this time from 21st on the grid!) as well as claiming victory in the other United States Grand Prix, held at Long Beach, Watson could fairly claim to be 'king of the streets'.

TYRRELL ON DETROIT

We were told before we first went to Detroit what an awful place it was going to be. That is not my experience: I think it is an excellent race circuit. The drivers complain about it being bumpy, but it is after all a street race. It brings out something quite different in cars and drivers and is tremendously demanding on both. There are many slow corners, many of them taken in second gear, which makes it very hard on transmissions and also tough on brakes. The driver is travelling between concrete walls the whole time; there is very little opportunity for anyone to overtake and no opportunity for the driver to relax. The paddock is outstanding but the teams have to drag all their equipment from there to the pits. Having to rush back to the paddock to get something which has been forgotten turns what normally is a chore into a nightmare And with the pits uncovered you hope like hell it's not going to rain!

For the 1986 event it was hot and dry, but with a strong breeze. The race had been preceded by practice sessions in which several drivers had discovered just how unrelenting are the concrete walls surrounding the circuit. Among those who had come to grief was Alain Prost, who had earlier admitted he hates the place – an opinion in marked contrast with his feeling for the other city-street GP, Monaco, where in 1986 he took his third successive victory.

Nigel Mansell arrived in Motown riding high, confident of achieving his third win in succession and looking capable of it during qualifying. He comfortably made the front row of the grid, though he had to concede pole to Senna's Lotus.

Though disappointed that France had just beaten Brazil in the World Cup, Senna took his own private revenge in the race, beating French driver Jacques Laffite's Ligier by a handsome margin. The Brazilian ace pulled off this win despite an early setback, for after only 14 laps he had to make an unscheduled call at the pits with a puncture, dropping from first to seventh. Despite this reverse he climbed steadily back through the field, regained the lead just before two-thirds of the distance, and strode to his second win of the season. For Mansell it was a sad day. After three laps he had his Williams in the lead, but shortly afterwards experienced a brake problem which made life really difficult – all the more so because the brake performance was not merely bad but inconsistently so. Sometimes he had brakes; other times the pedal went to the floor with little effect. Gradually he slid down the leader board, fell behind Alboreto's Ferrari when he had to make a hurried trip up an escape road, and eventually ended in fifth place.

Before Senna grabbed the lead, which he was to hold to the finish, he had been dogging fellow Brazilian Nelson Piquet. But after both had made tyre stops on successive laps Piquet crashed his Williams heavily into an outside wall. The stranded car, its front suspension destroyed, was at the exit from a blind corner: a really dangerous place. Race officials dithered, failed to remove the stricken car and after a few laps stopped hanging out warning flags so that drivers wrongly assumed that the course had been cleared. Senna came through and just missed the parked Williams, but René Arnoux hit it a glancing blow with his Ligier. The fiery Frenchman decided he could continue, but in doing so he became entangled with Thierry Boutsen's Arrows, putting both of them out of the race.

It was not the most impressive display of expertise by the organisers, who still had something to learn about running a grand prix. Maybe they should call in John Watson as honorary adviser.

Above *Nelson Piquet's Williams-Honda is (at last) lifted out of the way after it had partly blocked a dangerous left-hander for several minutes. Piquet had led briefly at the half-way stage, but then crashed immediately after completing the fastest lap (41) while defending his lead against Senna. Only 10 of the 29 starters were still going at the finish.*

Right *Winner Senna, Laffite (left) and Alain Prost, who took third place in spite of a repeat of the engine cut-out problems he had endured the previous week at Montreal – and of his well-known dislike of the Detroit circuit.*

GOODYEAR
DeLonghi
NACIONAL
RENAULT
Ford
Shell
BOSS

PROVENCE AND PASTIS

FRENCH GRAND PRIX

Mansell Makes It Three

Opposite page *Paul Ricard circuit was shortened after Elio de Angelis's fatal crash there while he was testing his Brabham-BMW BT55 two months before the French Grand Prix. The new first corner is seen here at bottom right; the pits are at top right.*

Left *Heavy traffic: Alain Prost (1) exits stage left, pursued by Johnny Dumfries (Lotus-Renault 98T), Nelson Piquet (6) and Jacques Laffite (26); Patrick Tambay (16) is taking a very tight line in a Lola-Ford THL2.*

As we have seen, the French Grand Prix is the daddy of them all, first staged way back in 1906 over public roads to the east of Le Mans.

Since then the French Grand Prix has been held on a variety of circuits all over the country. From 1950, when the F1 world championship was inaugurated, it has been staged at Reims, Rouen, Clermont-Ferrand, Le Mans, Dijon, and the Paul Ricard circuit which is currently its settled home. For those who witnessed grand prix racing over the course set in open fields outside Reims, with its tremendously fast Thillois straight, or thrilled to the downhill swerves after the pits at Rouen, or relished the dramatic setting of the Clermont-Ferrand circuit, the Paul Ricard circuit is pretty tame. It was built when there were strong moves for increased safety for both drivers and spectators, and the result is bland and clinical. It takes its name after the pastis magnate who financed it, though it is sometimes called Le Castellet, after the small village close by. A number of top drivers gave advice on its design, and even that prominent battler for safety, Jackie Stewart, gave it his approval.

When it opened Paul Ricard was hailed as the ultimate in safe design. The only thing lacking was atmosphere; and with spectators kept well away from the action and the Mediterranean shimmering not far away, it is hardly surprising that many people prefer to go to the beach instead of hauling their way up to the circuit in the hot month of July.

In spite of all the expert advice the track began to reveal deficiencies in the 1980s as cars became more powerful and faster. There was a near-tragic incident when two cars touched at the end of the very long Mistral straight, sending one flying through the air into what had been regarded as a safe crowd enclosure. Both drivers escaped serious injury, but a number of spectators were slightly hurt, and people were beginning to look more critically at this purportedly 'super safe' circuit. Then, in practice for the 1985 French Grand Prix, Nigel Mansell survived the fastest ever Formula 1 accident when a tyre burst as he approached the corner at the end of the straight at 200 mph. Mansell's car hit a catch-fence pole, which sent a front wheel flying backwards to strike his helmet. Mansell suffered serious concussion, but recovered in time for the British Grand Prix a fortnight later.

It was the fatal accident to Elio de Angelis in May 1986 (he was testing his Brabham at the time) that jerked the sporting authority into drastic action. The accident happened at 175 mph at the high-speed esses after the pits and

TYRRELL ON PAUL RICARD

From my point of view this is probably the least interesting circuit in the whole grand-prix series. It is just wide open spaces with little character. It could do with some gradients to make it more interesting, as at Spa. Admittedly, the race organisers shortened the circuit for the 1986 Grand Prix, so that the spectators were able to see the cars more often. But for the racing teams the circuit's only saving grace is that facilities in the pits and paddock are good.

within days it was announced that the circuit was to be modified for the French Grand Prix only a few weeks later. It seemed that the circuit was not only unexciting for spectators but unsafe as well.

The length was trimmed from 3.6 to 2.4 miles, cutting out the section where de Angelis was fatally injured and almost halving the Mistral straight; despite this, cars still reached terminal velocity going into the sweeping Signes right hander. There were pre-race worries that the new first corner would produce a pile up on the opening lap as 26 cars funnelled their way in. In the event there was less chaos than expected, though one or two of the back markers made minor contacts.

Nigel Mansell picked up his third victory in four races and owed it to a bold decision by Williams designer Patrick Head (in charge at the circuit in the absence of Frank Williams) to bring his cars in twice for fresh tyres. He reasoned, correctly as it turned out, that his cars would have an advantage on fresh tyres which would more than outweigh time spent twice in the pits; the strategy hinged on the ability of the Williams mechanics to get the cars re-shod in around eight seconds. The ploy worked perfectly for Mansell who, after his second call at the pits, set off about nine seconds behind leader Alain Prost. It did not take many laps for Mansell to catch and overtake the McLaren and stride on to victory.

The French may have been organising grands prix longer than anyone else but they hardly covered themselves with glory in 1986. During practice they allowed cars to continue running even with marshals all over the track trying to clear up oil dropped by blown engines. Then during the race there was pure farce as marshals made inept attempts to put out a blaze in Philippe Streiff's Tyrrell, which he parked conveniently just before the pit-lane entrance. The sorry episode culminated in the fire truck travelling the wrong way up the pit lane, and finally getting to the scene where the pipe carrying the extinguisher fluid flew off. By the time the fire had been put out the Tyrrell was gutted. After all the publicity and effort following the de Angelis accident one would have thought the French could have done better than this.

Main picture *Philippe Streiff's Tyrrell-Renault 015 fire, caused by a disconnected fuel line, occurred near the entrance to the pit lane. The inept performance of the marshals and the fire-fighting units made a mockery of France's 80-year experience in running grands prix.*

Far right *Both Nigel Mansell and Alain Prost ran on low turbocharger boost to conserve fuel. The Williams-Honda was clearly the happier on its frugal diet, Mansell beating the world champion by 17 seconds, with Nelson Piquet another 20 seconds adrift to take third place.*

canon
DENIM
Mobil 1
HONDA
ICI
Tactel
Mobil
5
GOODYEAR
canon

THE BEST OF BRANDS

Masterful Mansell: Luckless Laffite

Set in rolling Kent countryside some 20 miles south-east of London, Brands Hatch holds the strong affection of thousands of race fans. It is a circuit which evolved gradually from its origins as a motorcycle grass-track venue in the 1920s. After the war, the short, kidney-shaped track, set in a natural bowl that affords ideal viewing for the crowds, was given a cinder surface for the motorcyclists; then in 1950 (the year which saw the start of the Formula 1 World Championship) it was covered with tarmac to enable it to hold events for small-capacity single-seat racers. One of the entrants at the inaugural meeting was a fresh-faced Stirling Moss, then only 20 years old.

The circuit was extended to 1.24 miles in 1954, when it was switched to run clockwise. Six years later the grand prix extension was opened to bring it up to 2.65 miles, incorporating several tricky corners, changing cambers and gradients calling for the maximum of concentration. The first British Grand Prix was held there in 1964, when Jim Clark won in a Lotus–Climax, and Brands Hatch alternated with Silverstone as the grand prix host, though Brands supremo John Webb managed to slip in world-championship races, dubbed the European Grand Prix, in 1983, 1984 and 1985.

There was eager anticipation before the 1986 British Grand Prix, for Nigel Mansell had won three of the four previous championship rounds (and, moreover, had picked up his first-ever Formula 1 victory in the European Grand Prix a year earlier at the Kent track).

The crowds turned up in their thousands for the two practice days, when Frank Williams made his first public appearance since his road accident four months earlier, looking frail but mentally active and keeping a close eye on his team. Frank had reason to be pleased with what he saw, for his two cars were established on the front row of the grid, though Mansell fans were a little disappointed that Nelson Piquet had pipped him for pole.

It was hot and dry for race day and an estimated 120,000 spectators packed the roads for miles around as they queued for the car parks, some carrying banners urging their Nigel to show the rest a clean pair of heels. Though dissatisfied not to be on pole Mansell knew that his starting

Below *The pile-up at Paddock Corner mostly affected the back markers on the grid. From left to right: Stefan Johansson (28) is clear; then come Andrea de Cesaris (Minardi, 23), Piercarlo Ghinzani (Osella, 21), Thierry Boutsen (Arrows) and Jonathan Palmer (Zakspeed); chief victim, Jacques Laffite, is invisible.*

Right *René Arnoux (Ligier-Renault JS27) took a creditable fourth place.*

Shell Oils
DENIM
BOSS
Isle of Man
Mobil
1
DENIM
PMG
Mansell
Shell
BOSS
McLAREN INTERNATIONAL

TYRRELL ON BRANDS HATCH

From the crowd's point of view this is one of the best circuits in the world. It is a wonderful place to watch the cars, and it almost always produces an exciting motor race. It is very difficult to set up a car to give optimum performance here. You simply *must* have a well-balanced car at Brands, otherwise you are not going to be in the picture. And it's a driver's circuit, too, with several challenges. Paddock Bend is a spectacular and difficult corner because it is approached at high speed, and then the road falls away as the cars go down the hill. By modern standards the facilities for the teams are not top class, but there is always a tremendous atmosphere.

Left *An exhausted, almost dehydrated Nigel Mansell takes an early shower with plain water. His prospects were transformed by the race re-start – but the spare car he swopped for his own had not been furnished with a drink bottle.*

position on the left of the grid, which slopes from left to right, should give him better traction off the line.

The Williams duo were clearly favourites, but which driver would prevail? As the starting lights on the gantry flashed to green the pack roared away in a cloud of rubber smoke . . . and within a matter of yards, as Mansell snicked into second gear, a driveshaft coupling broke. His British Grand Prix was over almost before it had begun, or so it seemed.

But as he went into Paddock Bend with drive to only one wheel, all hell broke out behind him. A car suddenly veered out of control, setting in train a multiple accident in which several others were damaged and poor Jacques Laffite, the popular French veteran, was pinned in his blue Ligier after it went head on into a barrier on the inside of the track. More than half an hour passed before Laffite could be released and taken to hospital with serious leg and pelvic injuries.

Since the action had been stopped within two laps, the first start was declared null and void and the race began from scratch after a delay of nearly an hour and a half. It was a somewhat depleted field though some drivers had been able to switch to spare cars. Among them was Mansell, who took over the spare Williams, which had been set up for Piquet (who had tried the car briefly during practice and had not been happy with it).

While getting accustomed to his new mount, Mansell drove cautiously while team-mate Piquet led the field. Three laps gone and now feeling more confident with the car, Mansell had got up to second – and the team-mates began a battle that would last for some 190 miles.

The rest of the field were simply nowhere as the two Williams drivers fought bitterly, never more than a couple of seconds apart. The partisan crowd(and who could blame them with a British driver in the duel?) was urging Mansell on. On lap 23 of the 75-lap race, when Piquet missed a gear, he zoomed through to snatch the lead. Each made a tyre change stop in a goodish, if not brilliant, nine seconds plus, but Mansell clung to his lead to the finish, setting a new lap record as he kept Piquet at bay.

It was an exhausted Mansell who went up to the winner's rostrum to waste an expensive bottle of champagne over the massed fans below. The car he had driven so brilliantly was not fitted with a drink bottle, which meant he was thoroughly dehydrated. But he had won four out of the last five races and now led the drivers' championship.

All in all it was a great treat for the spectators. There is now a rule that GP winners forego the traditional lap of honour, but Mansell ignored this and toured the circuit, perched on a Range Rover, to a tremendous reception. He could be forgiven a breach of the regulations in his hour of triumph.

NOT LIKE THE OLD 'RING

McLaren Misjudge: Piquet Pounces

Opposite page *The cars were scarcely off the Hockenheim grid when Philippe Alliot (Laffite's Ligier replacement) hit the rear of Johansson's Ferrari, which in turn smacked into Teo Fabi's Benetton. Fabi retired at once; Johansson continued after repairs, but was in no mood to smile about it; Alliot retired after 11 laps.*

Below *Ayrton Senna (Lotus-Renault 98T) and Keke Rosberg (McLaren-TAG MP4/2C) fight for the lead, followed by back-marker Philippe Streiff (Tyrrell-Renault 015), shortly before Streiff retired with engine failure after 7 laps.*

Ken Tyrrell has said it all (see panel). Hockenheim does attract the crowds, but it hardly bears comparison with Brands Hatch as an exciting grand-prix venue. On Formula 1 day the grandstands are filled with about 60,000 spectators. There are, in fact, two smaller tribunes out in the country, but the majority of fans congregate round the stadium, and what goes on elsewhere can be seen only on TV.

The Grand Prix was first held at Hockenheim (some 10 miles south of Mannheim) in 1970, but returned to the old Nürburgring, south of Bonn, for the following six years, before going back to Hockenheim. It has been run there ever since, apart from 1985, when the race was staged at the expensively built new Nürburgring – which most enthusiasts regarded as a flop and showed their disapproval by staying away.

Hockenheim originally gained its reputation (and considerable popularity) as a venue for the now defunct Formula 2. It was in one of these races in 1968 that the great Jim Clark lost his life in a still unexplained crash. There was another nasty incident there during practice for the 1982 Grand Prix when Didier Pironi crashed his Ferrari in teeming rain and suffered serious injuries which put him out of racing.

There was an incident at the start of the 1986 Grand Prix, which saw Teo Fabi's Benetton and Stefan Johansson's Ferrari broadside across the track facing different directions. Fabi was an instant retirement while Johansson and Philippe Alliot (Ligier) had to call at the pits for attention. Fortunately there were no injuries.

On the eve of the race Keke Rosberg, the popular Finn who took the drivers' championship in 1982, announced that he would retire at the end of the season – and just to show he meant to bow out with a flourish he grabbed pole position for McLaren. Team-mate Prost was only fractionally slower, but they both feared the power/fuel-consumption ratio of the Honda-powered Williams pair. The race proved that fear well-founded, for Nelson Piquet was a clear

TYRRELL ON HOCKENHEIM

The present track was commissioned in 1966, since when three chicanes have been added to slow the cars on the long, high-speed straights. The pits are well-planned, but somehow the place has none of the atmosphere of the old Nürburgring. Almost all the spectators are crammed into the huge concrete stands in the so-called stadium area, where they can see only about one third of the circuit – a section where it is almost impossible to overtake. No, not a very interesting circuit for either the drivers or the public.

winner even though he permitted himself the luxury of a second pit stop for a further change of tyres.

For Mansell it was a day of frustration. He soon realised that his car was handling badly and found he had to concentrate furiously just to keep it on the tarmac. There was no way he was going to win this race.

Rosberg drove with his customary panache, leading for a number of laps on three occasions, but well aware that if he turned up his boost control too far he would risk running out of fuel. Prost, too, faced the same dilemma.

Piquet took the lead for the last time with five laps to go. Going into the final lap the order was Piquet, Rosberg and now Senna ahead of Prost and Mansell. The scribes in the press tribune were already working out the new drivers' championship placings when they had to tear up the figures as Rosberg coasted to a halt at the first chicane. So it was now Senna second; but he, too, was clearly low on fuel, weaving about to draw up the last drops from his tank. He just made it, but Prost was not so fortunate: whereas at Imola his fuel calculations proved inch-perfect (to coin a phrase), this time the TAG engine in his McLaren coughed dry with two corners to go.

The tough little Frenchman freewheeled slower and slower out of the last corner, the finishing line in sight. He undid his seat belts and jerked his body backwards and forwards in an effort to give added momentum. Then, realising he would not make it, he jumped out and began to push his car, as the crowd urged him on. It was typical of his competitive spirit – but he gave up when he remembered that pushing a car across the line no longer counts. So he was classified fifth and Rosberg sixth, a lap behind the winner, while Mansell profited from their misfortune to capture a fortunate third place and four valuable points. The McLaren pair could not hide their disappointment. They had both played it safe, driving with great prudence, and their computer read-outs had assured them they would make the race distance. This time, though, the boffins got it wrong.

Right *Nelson Piquet (Williams-Honda) achieved a well-earned second victory of the season by his finely judged decisions on tyre changes. He finished 15 seconds ahead of Ayrton Senna (Lotus-Renault) and almost 45 ahead of Nigel Mansell.*

Left *The McLaren drivers were both let down by their fuel-computer read-outs after driving prudent races. Keke Rosberg's car coughed to a halt at the first chicane on the last lap. Prost, seen here, ran dry when lying third with just two corners to go. He got out and started to push the car before remembering that this method of crossing the finishing line is no longer allowed.*

BEYOND THE IRON CURTAIN

Brazilians' Bitter Battle

__Below__ The first Hungarian Grand Prix for 50 years was held on a brand-new circuit about nine miles east of Budapest. The circuit was not much liked by the drivers: although set in rolling countryside, it was almost as slow and twisty as Monaco or Detroit. In the picture Ayrton Senna (Lotus-Renault 98T) is about to overtake the Zakspeed 861 of Dutchman Huub Rothengatter.

A few years ago there were preliminary moves to hold a grand prix in Moscow. As it turned out, it was Hungary which in 1986 staged the first world championship race beyond the Iron Curtain. Fifty years before, there had been a Hungarian Grand Prix, in a park in Budapest, won by the great Tazio Nuvolari in an Alfa Romeo. The long interval between the two races had certainly whetted the appetites of Hungarians, who recalled that it was one of their compatriots, Ferenc Szisz, who had won the first-ever grand prix 80 years earlier.

Any doubts about the ability of the organisers to stage a world championship race were soon dispelled as hordes of the media descended on the brand-new Hungaroring circuit some 12 miles from the capital, near the village of Mogyorod. It had been built in double-quick time: work had not begun until October 1985 and had been disrupted by a more than usually severe winter; but it was ready in time for a national meeting which tuned up the organisation in preparation for the grand prix in August.

For many journalists and commentators it was a first experience of a sphere of Soviet influence, but despite the inevitable officialdom, which meant snail-like progress with passports and visas at the airport and luggage turning up in unexpected places, there was a clear intention to provide a friendly welcome for visitors.

Budapest still shows some scars of the uprising 30 years earlier, with some buildings pock-marked with bullet holes, but the centre of the twin city on the banks of the Danube has a prosperous air, with luxury hotels from the international chains. The road from the city to the Hungaroring is a modern motorway, Hungary's M3, which on race day was as crowded as our own M3 on a bank holiday.

Drivers had a preliminary reconnaissance session to test the new track and the general opinion was that facilities were excellent but that the

track was too slow, the newly-laid surface placing a premium on grip. One driver described it as a street circuit without the houses. As originally planned it would have been quicker, but the discovery of an underground spring meant building a twisty section instead of a fast downhill sweep after the second corner. There were complaints of few overtaking opportunities, which are confined essentially to the entry to the corner at the end of the main straight, but it was generally agreed that the organisers had spent their estimated £5 million pretty well. For us, the crush of media representatives meant some overcrowding and the communications system was prone to wilt under the pressure.

In spite of the problems, however – which also included an understandable lack of marshalling experience – this was without doubt a propitious historic occasion, and the locals turned up in force even though the price of admission was more than half the national average weekly wage. Race day saw the highest attendance, estimated variously at between 140,000 and 200,000, at any sports event in the country's history. And they got their money's worth from a tense all-Brazilian struggle for victory.

Senna had snatched pole for Lotus and Piquet had his Williams alongside on the front of the grid. They were to be the two main contestants. Nigel Mansell was on the second row together with Prost's McLaren. Mansell had just announced that he had signed for the Williams

Left *A view from the hospitality area overlooking the pit lane on the Hungaroring. The race organization and facilities were well up to the F1 standard expected.*

team for the next two years (after strong rumours that he would drive for Ferrari) but in the race he was a far from happy contender. During practice Piquet had enjoyed the luxury of having use of the team's spare car, and he discovered that using a different type of differential gave an advantage on the slippery track surface. It was information he kept strictly to himself and his mechanics, and it was hardly surprising that Mansell was annoyed at being outsmarted by his team-mate. Neither could it have pleased Frank Williams, who had made his first trip abroad to watch a grand prix since his March accident. Mansell finished third; and although he retained his championship lead he knew he would have to keep a close eye on Piquet in the five races to come.

Senna stormed into the lead from the start, with Mansell trailing him, but after only three laps Piquet took advantage of his better-handling machine to slip into second place. After that it was an all-Brazilian battle, with Mansell losing ground all the time so that, at the finish, which came a lap sooner than scheduled because of the slowness of the track, he was a lap behind.

The spectators could not have cared less, for they revelled in the struggle up front. Piquet took over after 12 laps, then lost the lead to Senna when he pitted for fresh tyres, and he was still behind after Senna had made his tyre stop several laps later. But the superior straight-line speed of the Williams could not be denied and, after one desperate overtaking effort at the first corner, which almost succeeded, Piquet took the lead two laps later with a courageous effort which came very near to disaster.

After that there was nothing Senna could do but settle for second place. With Mansell third, Johnny Dumfries fifth for Lotus and Martin Brundle sixth in a Tyrrell there were three British drivers in the top six: quite a showing for the Union Jack. But the result was soured by that over-the-top degree of rivalry between the Williams drivers.

Right *The most exciting feature of the race was the struggle for first and second places between the Brazilian aces, Nelson Piquet eventually prevailing by 17 seconds. Senna's team-mate, Johnny Dumfries, got his first points of the season with a skilfully taken fifth place.*

TYRRELL ON HUNGARORING

This brand-new circuit got a wonderful reception from the public. The crowd are a long way from the action but they seemed to like it. At least they went in their numbers. It is a very slow circuit – the slowest of the non-street races by a long way – but it is an excellent modern facility and I found it a most interesting track. Drivers complained that it was too slow but I think a circuit like this serves a purpose. The beauty of grand-prix racing is the variation in the type of circuits, and I think there's a place for a circuit like Hungary's in the calendar.

SPEED AND SKILL AT ZELTWEG

Berger Brilliant: Prost Prevails

Below Michele Alboreto, ostensibly Ferrari's number one driver, would trail team-mate Stefan Johansson by 14 points to 23 at the end of the season. But at Zeltwig he achieved his, and Ferrari's, highest placing in 1986, finishing second; Johansson followed him home in third place to complete a good day's work for Maranello.

The first Austrian Grand Prix counting for the World Championship was held in 1964 on a makeshift course laid out with straw bales on the aerodrome at Zeltweg (about 30 miles west-north-west of Graz), which was 'borrowed' for the event. Conditions were primitive, with a retired London bus housing the timekeepers and the press located in a hastily erected marquee in the centre of the track. The circuit was extremely bumpy and played havoc with the cars, one driver after another retiring as their machinery took a fearful hammering. The Italian driver Lorenzo Bandini pulled off a surprise by winning for Ferrari. The airfield circuit was clearly not good enough and the next Austrian World Championship GP had to await the building of the magnificent Österreichring, only a short distance from Zeltweg.

The circuit has staged every Austrian GP since 1970 and has produced some thrilling races. With its straights and long curves it is frighteningly fast and calls for tremendous driving skill as well as sheer courage.

Bandini's win was his first (and only) grand-prix victory, and since then the Austrian event has been notable for the number of drivers who have notched their first GP success. There was Vittorio Brambilla, who won a rain-shortened race in 1975 (and in his euphoria damaged his March on his victory lap); John Watson, who scored for Penske in 1976; Alan Jones, who picked up the first of his 12 GP wins in 1977; and Elio de Angelis, who scorched across the line in a breathtaking finish just five-hundredths of a second ahead of prospective champion Keke Rosberg in 1982.

The 1986 race looked like producing another first-time winner, for during qualifying the two Benetton drivers, Teo Fabi and local hero Gerhard Berger, had used the impressive top-end power of their BMW engines to dominate and take the front row of the grid. When the race began they rushed away from the opposition, though Fabi, the serious little Italian, soon knew he was destined for early retirement after his car bottomed so hard that it jumped out of third gear and he over-revved the engine. He did nose ahead

TYRRELL ON ÖSTERREICHRING

This has become one of the classic circuits. With a substantial backdrop of wooded hills, it has a really beautiful setting. It draws much of its strength, as far as spectators are concerned, by being close to the Italian border, and so attracts a lot of Italians. It has seen some memorable races and very close finishes. And it is one of the few circuits where my team has never won a grand prix!

Right *Gerhard Berger (Benetton-BMW B186) leaves Philippe Streiff's Tyrrell-Renault 015 behind. Berger and his team-mate Teo Fabi (pole position) led for the first 16 laps. After a lengthy pit stop Berger fought back to seventh place, making the fastest lap on his home circuit.*

of Berger for a brief moment on lap 17, but almost immediately afterwards his race was over.

The Austrian fans cheered on Berger, hoping he would emulate Niki Lauda, who had won his home grand prix in 1984. Berger's Benetton was on hard Pirelli tyres and there were rumours that he intended to complete the race without changing them. But just before half distance he came into the pits: he did take on fresh tyres but this was only routine while mechanics tried frantically to track down an engine misfire. He had lost three laps before the trouble was found to be a flat battery, and although he vented his frustration by driving faster than anyone else on the circuit he could finish only seventh.

Disconsolate Austrians began to drift to the car parks as Berger's chances disappeared in the pits and Mansell took over the lead. It was not long, though, before Prost headed the field, and he went on to his 24th grand-prix victory, although not without a late crisis. With Keke Rosberg holding second place there seemed every prospect of a McLaren one-two. But with a few laps to go the Finn was in trouble as his engine persistently cut out; and finally it died on him. Prost was having similar difficulty with this fault, which was no stranger to the TAG engine. The signs were ominous, with the engine cutting out not only as he slowed for corners but also in the straight. However, Prost just managed to coax his ailing car home.

Although many Austrians had left the circuit, the thousands of Italian fans were going wild in the closing laps, sensing that Michele Alboreto and Stefan Johansson might catch the ailing McLaren and come first and second for Ferrari. But it was not to be. For Johansson this was a race which called on all his physical resources and determination. He had had a serious accident on the first practice day when he rammed an advertising hoarding and he was in considerable pain. The next day his brakes played up and he hit a barrier, which did nothing to improve his condition. He drove a fine race to finish third in a state of agony.

It was a bad day for the 'Gang of Five'. Only Prost was there at the finish; Senna and Piquet went out with engine trouble, Mansell walked home after a driveshaft broke, and Rosberg came to a halt with only five laps to go.

With four rounds to go Mansell still headed the championship table, but Prost was now breathing down his neck, only two points adrift, while Senna and Piquet were still strongly in contention.

Below *Alain Prost (McLaren-TAG MP4/2C) at last returned to winning ways, scoring his third victory of the season – but his first for eight races. Here he is hunted by Nigel Mansell (Williams-Honda FW11), who retired after 32 laps.*

NO JOY FOR THE TIFOSI

Williams Give 'Em the Old 1–2

Apart from 1980, when it was held at Imola, the Italian Grand Prix has always been at Monza since the World Championships began in 1950. The original circuit goes back much further, to 1922, when the first Italian GP was run there.

The race-crazy *tifosi* adore Monza, built in a huge royal park a few miles north of Milan. They swarm there in their thousands, waving large Ferrari flags and ready to cheer their favourite red cars. The police have a tremendous job keeping control, and despite their efforts they cannot prevent some spectators getting into the circuit without paying – holes in the tough fencing bearing witness to the use of wire cutters. Excited fans have even ventured on to the track before the race has ended, endangering both themselves and drivers. That is why the organisers now draft in a large number of vicious guard dogs, their handlers instructed to stop at nothing to keep the track clear until the finish.

After that there is complete chaos which nothing but an armoured corps could prevent. The crowds mill all over, snitching anything they can lay their hands on in the paddock. Discarded racing tyres are carried off by triumphant youngsters, and everyone has to keep a tight hold on wallets. Over the years many a journalist has lost money and documents. The tunnel underneath the track between the grandstand and the paddock is a happy hunting ground for pickpockets. Yes, it's a wild place to be: I once saw police vainly firing their pistols at thieves escaping from the press car park.

The thieves are nothing if not enterprising. On one occasion fans arriving on motorcycles were persuaded to leave their machines in a large van which the 'owner' said would be locked during the race. They happily handed over their lire for the promise of safe keeping. The van *was* locked when it was full . . . then driven off with its load. Needless to say, the van had been stolen, too!

None of this deters the Italian fans, who are thoroughly wound up by the media coverage which, in both extent and excitability, far exceeds that given to motor-sport in Britain. There is always a tremendous TV build up to arouse interest, inevitably centred on local drivers and, above all, on the Ferrari drivers, whatever their nationality. Pre-race ticket sales were, in fact,

Below *Oz ace Alan Jones, who took the 1980 drivers' title with Williams, was piloting the much less competitive Lola-Ford THL2 in 1986, teaming up with Patrick Tambay. He followed up his splendid non-stop fourth place at Zeltweg with an excellent sixth place at Monza – in spite of having handling problems after losing a wheel weight.*

TYRRELL ON MONZA

Facilities for the teams at Monza are the most primitive of the permanent circuits. The pits are old and just about big enough to hold a toolbox! There is always a big problem with the crowds. In spite of the fencing they invariably find a way through into the paddock after the race has finished (and some of them even before), so there is a mad rush to get all our equipment in behind closed doors. The racing was much closer before they brought in the chicanes – we often saw two, three, even four cars going over the finishing line together. We don't see that now. Nevertheless, I think it is quite an interesting circuit and there is something special about racing at Monza because of its tradition. It is very hard on brakes and very heavy on fuel consumption, but it's a relatively easy circuit for a driver because, apart from two places, it is really all straights and chicanes.

Below *The fanatical* tifosi *are endlessly resourceful in their pursuit of vantage points, constructing personal grandstands in the timber.*

***Right** Stefan Johansson (Ferrari F186) passes under Monza's famous Campari ad., which rivals the Dunlop 'bridge' at Le Mans as a circuit landmark. Johansson sent the fickle* tifosi *home reasonably contented after taking third spot.*

down for the 1986 Grand Prix, owing partly to a huge increase in admission and partly to the fact that Ferrari looked to have little chance of winning, especially as Michele Alboreto was reported to be unwell.

Teo Fabi had his Benetton on pole position for the second successive race, with Prost alongside in his McLaren. It was a front row which melted before the start in a unique chain of incidents. Both Fabi and Prost failed to get away for the warm-up lap. Fabi eventually got going, but was obliged to begin the race from the back of the grid. Prost, his battery flat, sprinted to the pits to switch to his spare car. He started his race from the pits, so that effectively Mansell and Berger were the new front row.

Both Fabi and Prost soon began to scythe through the field. Fabi eventually had to retire towards the end, and Prost, after a brilliant display of aggressive driving, which at one time got him up to fifth position, was black-flagged for changing cars after the green flag had signalled the start of the formation lap. Prost was understandably displeased at such a late decision, having driven his heart out and taken chances for three-quarters of an hour, all for nothing. At least he retired honourably, after the half-way mark, with a blown engine after ignoring the black flag for a couple of laps.

The race turned into a Williams benefit. Mansell passed Berger to take the lead on lap 7, retained it until after his tyre change, but was overtaken on lap 38 by Piquet, who was clearly quicker on the day, having gambled successfully on a modified rear wing which gave him greater straight-line speed.

Mansell drove part of the race with a handicap. One of his seat belt webs came undone soon after his pit stop, making driving just that little bit more uncomfortable and less confident. The flag came down for Piquet with Mansell 10 seconds behind, a result which made sure the Williams team clinched the Constructors' World Championship. Rivals they might be, but Mansell applauded Piquet on their cooling-down lap and the Brazilian acknowledged with a salute.

And with Stefan Johansson bringing his Ferrari home third, it meant a lot of Italians went home happier than they had been when they set out for the circuit in the park.

Above *The Williams-Honda team reasserted itself with a vengeance at Monza, Nelson Piquet with his fourth victory of the season shading Nigel Mansell by less than 10 seconds.*

ESTORIL EXPRESS

PORTUGUESE GRAND PRIX

Mansell All the Way

Above *The pit lane at Estoril. In the foreground is the Williams pit; beyond it are the Lotus and Brabham pits. Williams provided each of their drivers with a race-ready spare car for the Portuguese race; Nelson Piquet had tested a fifth FW11 at the Silverstone circuit a few days before his departure for Portugal.*

Portugal has neither a long nor continuous tradition in grand-prix racing. The first World Championship race took place at Oporto in 1958, when Stirling Moss won in a Vanwall. The following year it was Moss first again with a Cooper-Climax on a circuit outside Lisbon. Then in 1960 it was back to Oporto when Jack Brabham took the flag in a Cooper-Climax.

After that Portugal was in the grand prix wilderness until 1984, when a new and hastily completed circuit set in the hills a few miles from the seaside resort of Estoril staged the fourth Portuguese Grand Prix. That race and the two which followed were all memorable in different ways.

The 1984 Grand Prix was ill-attended, for Portugal is still a poor country and the admission prices must have daunted most of the locals. But if the crowd was thin the media were present in force: it was the last race of the season and it was still to be decided which of the McLaren drivers, Alain Prost or Niki Lauda, would be world

Below *Alain Prost picked up crucial (if fortunate) extra points in taking second place after Senna, betrayed by an inaccurate computer read-out, ran out of fuel on the last lap.*

champion. It had been a year of McLaren domination. Prost won his seventh GP of the season in Estoril, yet by coming second Lauda pipped him for the title (his third) by just half a point – the closest margin ever. Lauda owed his title to Mansell, who lost a fine second place when his Lotus had sudden brake failure. If Mansell had come second, Prost would have been champion.

In 1985 there was another great race at Estoril. This time it was a demonstration of wet-weather driving the like of which is still talked of with bated breath. Under really diabolical conditions which caused several drivers, including the winner, to ask for the race to by stopped, Ayrton Senna produced a performance that left all his rivals standing. He led from start to finish in his Lotus and by the end had lapped all the field with the exception of Alboreto's Ferrari. It was a demonstration of instinctive skill that will go down as one of the greats of motor racing: Senna's first grand-prix victory, and the day he came of age.

When the teams went to Portugal in September 1986 four drivers were still in with a chance of capturing the World Championship: Mansell, Piquet, Prost and Senna. Tension was high and in an effort to show there was to be no favouritism in the Williams team, Mansell was given the luxury of a spare car, something his team-mate had enjoyed throughout the season. It clearly had an effect on Mansell's confidence, and though he was disappointed to be pipped for pole by Senna's Lotus, the Englishman was determined to increase his championship points lead by setting the pace from the start.

He did just that, pulling clear of Senna as they roared towards the right hander at the end of the straight and dominating the race throughout the whole 70 laps. No one could hold Mansell that day as he drove what was probably the finest race of his career, surpassing even his brilliant performance in the British GP. Senna put up a stalwart battle; but after trailing Mansell throughout, he ran out of fuel on the final lap to finish fourth, his hopes of the championship now dashed. Piquet's efforts to get on terms with Senna caused him to spin with a few laps to go. With Senna out of fuel, Prost finished second and Piquet third.

It was an inspired display by Mansell, which put him 10 points ahead of his nearest rival, Piquet, who in turn led Prost by one point. With two rounds to go prospects were beginning to look distinctly rosy for Mansell in his effort to become the first British world champion since James Hunt had taken the title in 1976.

But motor racing is littered with might-have-beens and the vagaries of chance, and with Mexico City and Adelaide to come the fates decided to spit on their hands and get down to business.

TYRRELL ON ESTORIL

I think this is a good circuit, a very interesting circuit. It has a little bit of everything – fast corners, slow corners and a longish straight. I've never quite understood why it fails to attract a good crowd. Facilities for the teams are good and I think most drivers enjoy driving there. They have the opportunity to think between corners, and this makes it a good circuit for testing.

Above *Sharing the front row of the grid with Ayrton Senna (pole), Nigel Mansell dominated the race from start to finish in perhaps his finest drive of the season.*

Right *The four contenders for the drivers' title pose before the Portuguese Grand Prix; from left, Ayrton Senna (fourth at Estoril), Alain Prost (second), Nigel Mansell (first), Nelson Piquet (third). The result in Portugal did little to resolve the issue: the fight for the drivers' championship would continue to the last race of the season.*

LONG TIME NO SEE

MEXICAN GRAND PRIX

Non-stop Berger's First Win

Below *Supporting roles at Mexico City: Alain Prost, seen here snapping at Ayrton Senna's heels, drove cannily to take second place with only one stop for tyres; Senna, who came third, was forced to pit twice, as was Nelson Piquet.*

During the 1960s the Mexican Grand Prix was a regular date in the calendar, but the 1970 race was such a dangerous shambles that it disappeared from the Formula 1 scene for 16 years. Jackie Stewart still shudders when he recalls that 1970 Grand Prix. It looked to have all the makings of a disaster, with excited spectators swarming everywhere, lining the verge of the circuit and even sitting on the track. Both Jackie and local hero Pedro Rodriguez repeatedly appealed for sanity, but to no avail. Reluctantly it was decided to stage the race: the organisers feared that if it was cancelled the huge crowd, estimated at close on 200,000, might riot. During the race Rodriguez nearly killed a youngster who scampered across the track, while Stewart hit a dog at high speed and only just managed to avoid ploughing into the crowd.

Despite the massive earthquake of 1985 which had caused tremendous damage and took a terrible toll of human life in a city already economically bankrupt the organisers went ahead with expensive preparations for the 1986 Mexican race. The circuit, a few miles from the centre of the sprawling capital, was completely modernised, some of the corners altered, and a new pits complex built in only a few months.

With the prospect of Nigel Mansell clinching the World Championship, representatives of the British media made a mass pilgrimage to Mexico City, which lies some 7,500 feet above sea level and is surely the smog capital of the world. No one knows exactly how many people live in the city, but it is thought at least 18 million and maybe more. The contrasts of affluence and poverty are frightening, the traffic horrendous, the hundreds of ruined buildings a sinister reminder of the quake.

The old circuit had been named after Ricardo Rodriguez, the younger of two brilliant Mexican brothers who was killed during practice for his native grand prix in 1962 at the age of 20. His brother, Pedro, also died in a racing accident in 1971, and the new circuit was renamed Autodromo Hermanos Rodriguez (Rodriguez Brothers Race Circuit).

Drivers agreed that the organisers had done a good job: there was no chance this time of track invasions by spectators. But there were other problems. The track was bumpy in parts and the surface abrasive. The altitude posed breathing problems for both drivers and cars, and most teams used larger turbochargers to force more of the thin air into the engines and fitted bigger radiators to aid cooling.

There was a further problem. It was difficult for visitors to escape the attentions of the local bugs. Some teams imported their own food and drinks, but in spite of precautions the dreaded 'Aztec Twostep' hit many. One of the victims was Mansell, who went to a party to celebrate the birthday of BBC commentator Murray Walker and was distinctly unwell on race day. Although he was on the second row of the grid, behind Senna and Piquet, the start of the race was a disaster for Mansell, who was unable to get into first gear and was left behind as the pack surged away. He was 18th at the end of lap 1 and

Below *Andrea de Cesaris achieved a creditable eighth place in achieving Minardi's first finish of the year – a minor triumph embellished by team-mate Alessandro Nannini's 14th place, two laps further back.*

Above *Gerhard Berger (Benetton-BMW B186) confirmed his reputation as a rising star by winning by a clear 25 seconds in Mexico. While his rivals were trying to work out when he would pit for a tyre change, Berger went serenely on, safely completing the 78 laps on his original rubber. Berger's triumph in Mexico clinched Ferrari's decision to offer him a team place for the 1987 season.*

TYRRELL ON MEXICO CITY

It was nice to have the grand-prix circus return to Mexico once more, and they had done a terrific job in modernising the facilities. There are quite a few changes from the track we knew in the 1960s, and it is now quite an interesting circuit. The problem for the teams is the altitude, although the performance of turbocharged cars is to some extent restored by the fact that they have forced induction. The local bugs are a problem for us Westerners, but it is possible to get by providing you are careful and perhaps a bit lucky.

although he charged through the field to reach ninth place the effort took severe toll of his tyres and he lost time with an unscheduled pit stop. He had to make another stop for more tyres later on and finished a disappointed fifth.

Meanwhile, his Williams team-mate, Piquet, looked like running away with the race: he led into the first corner and just before half distance he led from Senna, Prost, and Gerhard Berger. But then Piquet began to have tyre trouble and, after making three pit stops, had to be content with fourth place. Senna, too, was having trouble with his tyres, but made do with two stops to take third place. Typically, Prost saw this danger sooner than anyone and, with judicious driving, made do with one pit stop, taking second place in spite of a dodgy engine.

But the hero of the day was Berger, whose Benetton was the only one of the serious contenders to use Pirelli tyres (the others were on Goodyear). Using the hardest Pirelli compound on his left wheels to combat wear, the young Austrian managed to keep in touch with the leaders until they made their tyre stops, took the lead on lap 36 – and managed to complete the race on his original rubber, thanks also to a unique new British-designed differential. It was Berger's and Benetton's first Formula 1 victory.

So Mexico had failed to decide the championship. Three drivers – Mansell (70 points), Prost (64 points) and Piquet (63 points) – were still in the hunt with one round to go; Senna (55 points) was out of it. Adelaide would settle the issue.

Right *A future champion? Gerhard Berger savours his hour of triumph. Second-placed Alain Prost, who was hampered by a defunct cylinder, is at left; on the right is third-placed Ayrton Senna, who had achieved pole position on the grid for the eighth time in 15 races.*

SHOWDOWN IN ADELAIDE

Prost Champion Again

Below *Blast-off! The big four get away from the grid. From right to left, Nigel Mansell (who had snatched pole position), Ayrton Senna, Nelson Piquet (who took the other front-row berth), and Alain Prost (who shared the second row with Senna).*

There have been many races carrying the title of Australian Grand Prix, at many different venues and for many different racing categories, and the winners have included such greats as Jack Brabham, Stirling Moss, Bruce McLaren, Graham Hill, Jackie Stewart, Jim Clark, Alan Jones and Alain Prost. It was not, however, until 1985 that Australia got on to the Formula 1 World Championship calendar. It was preceded by intense inter-state rivalry but in the end, to the surprise of many, it was the outsider South Australia which won the day. The city of Adelaide went about organising the grand prix in a very businesslike way. Any misgivings the Formula 1 circus might have entertained about the city's ability to stage a championship race were quickly dispelled at the 1985 meeting. It was well promoted and every effort was made to put South Australia on the map. Sceptics from Europe were amazed at the efficiency of the organisation and the friendliness of everyone concerned.

They produced a real road circuit, set in the suburbs, part parkland, part city streets and part of a horse-racing track. Local interest was so great that touts were everywhere, offering money for spare entrance tickets. The 1985 Grand Prix had gone to Keke Rosberg in his last drive for the Williams team and experienced observers came back full of praise for what many thought the best organised race of the season.

For the 1986 Grand Prix the organisers had everything in their favour, especially the fact that it was a three-sided championship clincher for the drivers. There was Piquet out to take his third title, Prost poised to grab his second in succession, and Nigel Mansell looking for his first. No race organiser could ask for more. The BBC laid

on live coverage in the early hours of Sunday morning. The pre-race favourite had to be Mansell, for even if either of his two rivals won the race he could still pip them by finishing second or third.

Mansell knew what he had to do and drove a perfectly judged race. With 19 laps to go he was cruising along nicely in third place, headed by Piquet and Prost. Then came the drama, a scene repeated so often since on TV screens all over the world. With the Williams touching about 180 mph in sixth gear, Mansell's left rear tyre suddenly exploded. The situation had all the makings of a massive accident, but Mansell wrestled successfully as his car teetered on the edge of disaster. With his right front wheel high

TYRRELL ON ADELAIDE

This is definitely one of my favourites. The Australians did a fantastic job in setting up this grand prix. It is really a very interesting circuit. It is quite close to the city centre, has fine facilities and we've seen some wonderful motor racing there. It is very hard on the cars and transmissions. Like some other circuits it presents a problem in choosing between the right amount of downforce for cornering and for straight-line speed. For a street circuit it has a quite substantial straight, which is one of the few overtaking places.

Above *Tragedy for Nigel Mansell struck on lap 64, his left rear tyre exploding while he was approaching 180 mph on the main straight. Almost exactly the same thing had happened to Keke Rosberg two laps earlier – a sad way to end his great career in Formula 1.*

Left *Martin Brundle (Tyrrell-Renault 015) got among the points for the fourth time at Adelaide, where he recorded his highest placing (fourth) of the championship.*

off the ground he had steering only through the other front wheel. Somehow he managed to slow down and coax his stricken machine up the escape road where it bumped gently into a wall. He was lucky to be alive – but his championship hopes had exploded as decisively as his tyre.

A short while before Rosberg had retired with a tyre problem and, as a precaution, it was decided to bring in Piquet for fresh rubber. While he was in the pits Prost swooped past into the lead. Piquet pulled out all the stops in an effort to wrest back the lead, but despite a succession of fastest laps he failed by just over four seconds.

What Piquet did not know as he made his charge was that Prost was a very worried Frenchman. The fuel read out in his McLaren showed him he was due to run dry before the finish. Under normal circumstances Prost would have eased back to conserve his fuel and settle for second place. With the championship at stake this was out of the question. He had to gamble. He pressed on just fast enough to keep Piquet at bay – and became the first driver to take the title in successive years since Jack Brabham did it for Cooper in 1959 and 1960.

With hindsight it seemed that Prost may have owed his second title to a puncture. This had obliged him to make an unscheduled stop before half distance and while in the pits he got a complete set of new rubber – although investigation of the punctured tyre suggested to technicians that the original Goodyears ought to last the whole race. Without that puncture Prost might have had later tyre trouble.

So maybe there was an element of good fortune for Prost. But he had done the job in a way that underlined his dedicated approach. He was a worthy double champion and – in most people's eyes – the man the others had to beat.

Below Champion again! Alain Prost leaps with elation after taking first place. Rosberg and Mansell (who needed third place or better to take the title) had been in close contention until the race was three parts run. Piquet led after Mansell's drama, but his team manager wisely ordered him in for a tyre change. Prost was hunted remorselessly by Piquet in the closing laps, but he still had a four-second margin at the flag.

INDEX

Italic figures refer to the captions

Acknowledgements

The Publishers thank the following for providing the photographs in this book:

Allsport 126–7, 138–9, (Bruty) 72–3, (Gould) 186, 188–9; Allsport/Vandystadt 70–1, 73 inset, 76, 80, 108–9, 116–7, 123 inset, 150; Charles Briscoe-Knight 4–5, 52–3, 58, 61, 64–5, 67, 78 inset, 85, 87, 92–3, 111, 119, 122–3, 132–3, 146, 178–9; Diana Burnett 63, 84, 89, 103 inset, 105 inset, 106, 134–5, 137 inset, 144, 156, 187; Colorsport/SIPA (Brocard) 110–1, (Compoint) 50–1, 53, 104–5, 120–1, (Morvan) 96–7, (Ponomareff) 147, (Taillade) 114; Mirco Decet 15 above; D.P.P.I. 41, 128–9, 131, 135 inset, 148, 155, 158–9, (Gilles/Levent) 56–7, 94–5, (Guichaqua) 166, (Levent) 148–9, 180–1, 184–5, 188, (Levent/Vargioulu) 54–5, 62–3, 68, 86–7, (Vargioulu) 154, 170–1, 173; Geoffrey Goddard 12 below, 13, 14, 15 below, 18, 21 above, 22, 2, 32, 32–3, 33, 34–5, 38–9, 46, 47 above; Dave Kennard 90–1, 98–9, 139, 157 inset, 162, 168–9, 177, 178; McLaren International 6 inset, 6–7; L.A.T. Photographic Ltd. 2–3, 20 below, 30 below, 36–7, 39, 40, 41, 43, 44–5, 45, 48–9; Popperfoto 27, 30 above, 31, 35; Cyril Posthumus 17 below, 20 above; RAC 10–1; Peter Roberts Collection 8–9, 11, 12 above, 14 inset, 16, 17 above, 22–3, 28–9; Nigel Snowdon 42–3, 56, 60, 76–7, 78–9, 107, 130, 133, 163, 164, 167; Sporting Pictures 58–9, 69, 81, 82, 100, 100–1, 102–3, 115, 118–9, 136–7, 141, 143, 145, 172; Sutton Photographic 1, 66, 75, 88, 112–3, 120 inset, 129 inset, 140–1, 142, 151 inset, 152, 153, 159 inset, 160–1, 164–5, 174, 175, 176, 181 inset, 182–3, 183, 185; Bob Thomas Sports Photography 74–5, 124–5; Zoom Photographic 126.

Ian Dawson (Octopus Picture Library) 18–9, 24, 26–7

JACKET PICTURES Front cover Nigel Snowdon. Back cover: above left Colorsport/SIPA (Compoint); above right Allsport (Simon Bruty); below left Allsport/Vandystadt; below right Allsport/Vandystadt; bottom Allsport